The German Bachelor
&
the French Girl

The Story of Lewis & Marguerite (Clair) Rinn

Janelle Richardson

The German Bachelor & the French Girl
The Story of Lewis & Marguerite (Clair) Rinn

Copyright ©2021 Janelle Richardson

ISBN   978-0-578-84960-7 (Hardbound)
ISBN   978-0-578-84961-4 (Softcover)

All rights reserved. No part of this publication may be reproduced, distributed, or transmitted in any form or by any means, including photocopying, recording, or other electronic or mechanical methods, without the prior written permission of the publisher, except in the case of brief quotations embodied in critical reviews and certain other noncommercial uses permitted by copyright law.

Book design by StoriesToTellBooks.com

The German Bachelor
&
the French Girl

The Story of Lewis & Marguerite (Clair) Rinn

CONTENTS

Preface ... vii

PART I Lewis and Marguerite Together

Chapter 1
Lewis and Marguerite Meet ... 3

Chapter 2
Living at Camp Supply ... 7

Chapter 3
Moving to Kansas ... 12

Chapter 4
Breaking the Sod in Oklahoma ... 29

Chapter 5
Marguerite Holding Family Together ... 42

PART II Marguerite's Early Life

Chapter 6
Marguerite Clair Born in France ... 65

Chapter 7
Clairs Coming to America ... 74

Chapter 8
Living at Silkville Commune ... 82

PART III Lewis's Early Life

Chapter 9
Ludwig "Lewis" Rinn Born in Germany ... 92

Chapter 10
Rinns Coming to America ... 101

Chapter 11
    Lewis Rinn Going to War   107

Chapter 12
    Lewis Rinn Moving West   125

PART IV The Spirited Bunch: Lewis and Marguerite's Children

Chapter 13
    Lottie Benoite Rinn   130

Chapter 14
    Claire Louise Rinn   137

Chapter 15
    Daniel Claude Rinn   142

Chapter 16
    Violet Florene Rinn   150

Chapter 17
    Theoda Virginia Rinn   155

Chapter 18
    Lewis David Rinn   162

Chapter 19
    Edmond Valton Rinn   166

Chapter 20
    Seona Helen Rinn   172

Chapter 21
    Jessie Mae Rinn   180

PART V Not Forgotten: Rinn Family Gatherings

The Rinn Children   187

Rinn Descendants   188

Endnotes   191

Acknowledgements

Thanks to the many people who contributed to the creation of this book. Family members took the time to supply family pictures and stories and to offer their support.

When I began researching the Rinn family in 1994, I knew little about the family, so I contacted second cousin, JoAnn Gedosh. She put me in contact with another second cousin, the late Paula Phillips, who generously shared her earlier research.

Thanks to JoAnn Gedosh for organizing family reunions which were a source of inspiration and information. Over the years, family members shared many stories. At one reunion, I interviewed Bill Thompson and the late Don Daggs who recalled their memories. The late Gene Rinn, unable to attend a reunion and terminally ill, phoned to share his recollections.

Pictures were shared by Paula Phillips, Frances Grimes, Chris Eld, Steve Eld, JoAnn Gedosh, Bill Thompson, Gene Rinn, the Daggs family, Claude Jardon and others.

The late Scott Rinn made contact with Rinn family in Germany which lead to 18 family members visiting the German and French hometowns of Lewis and Marguerite (Clair) Rinn in 2000. He also wrote an account of his grandfather, Daniel Claude Rinn. The late Paula Phillips wrote the narrative of her grandmother, Claire Rinn. The description of Theoda Rinn was written by Bev Peavler and JoAnn Gedosh. Those accounts are in Part IV.

Bev Peavler reviewed early drafts. The San Luis Obispo County Genealogical Society Writing Group I reviewed later drafts. I am grateful for their support, suggestions and corrections.

My husband, Nereus "Nick" Richardson deserves special mention because he "bugged" me to complete the book, and he enabled me to have the resources to do so.

Thanks to all those I have not specifically named who made the completions of this book possible.

Preface

This book tells the story of Lewis and Marguerite (Clair) Rinn, my great-grandparents. Many years ago, I began gathering information about this couple until I accumulated many pictures, records, and stories. Eventually, I realized nobody would look at this information as long as it sat in my file cabinets. Their stories needed to be preserved or they would be gone forever. I needed to create a book containing more than a list of names, dates, and places.

Putting together the book was much more work than I first anticipated because I wanted to get it complete and "perfect." Finally, I realized the book would never be fully complete because family history is never complete, nor totally accurate. I needed to publish it regardless. I attempted to obtain correct information and cited the sources, but there are gaps, discrepancies, and very likely errors. Hopefully, family members will add to and correct this work.

The book begins with Part I focusing on "Lewis and Marguerite Rinn Together." It tells the story of the romance and unlikely marriage of an older German bachelor and a young French girl and their 29 years of marriage raising their nine children. The story begins at an army outpost in Indian Territory, progresses to Kansas and back to Oklahoma Territory. It ends with the death of Lewis Rinn and Marguerite holding the family together until her death.

Part II portrays "Marguerite Clair's Early Life." Her life began in France where her ancestors originated. When she was 12, her family left family and friends and came to Kansas to live in a commune. Not quite 19, she went to an army outpost in Indian Territory and her life changed forever.

"Ludwig "Lewis" Rinn's Early Life" is told in Part III. He was 12-years-old when his family left central Germany, sailed to America, and settled in Pittsburgh. As a young man, he joined the Union Army and served 3 years in the Civil War. After the war, he headed west and ended up in Indian Territory where he met Marguerite Clair.

Part IV describes "Their Children—the Spirited Bunch." An account of each of the nine children is given. The title, "Spirited Bunch" was taken from a conversation I had many years ago with an elderly woman attending the Minco, Oklahoma, High School Reunion. Knowing my Dad was part of the Rinn family, she told me she remembered Marguerite Rinn and her bunch of children. With a twinkle in her eyes, she smiled and said, "They were certainly a spirited bunch."

Pictures illustrate some of the family get-togethers in Part V "Not Forgotten—Rinn Family Reunions." Many family gatherings took place over the years as descendants gathered to remember and tell stories.

This book is intended to help preserve the story of Lewis and Marguerite (Clair) Rinn.

Janelle Richardson, Great-granddaughter

Morro Bay, California

2021

PART I

Lewis and Marguerite Together

"Papa was older than Mama and spoiled her. He worshipped the ground she walked on."

~Jessie Rinn, youngest daughter

Eighteen-year-old Marguerite Clair

Twenty-eight-year old Lewis Rinn

Marriage Certificate, Ford County, Kansas

Chapter 1

Lewis and Marguerite Meet

Lewis Rinn and Marguerite Clair married at Dodge City, Kansas, on Saturday, July 29, 1876.[1] Not all the details of their romance are known. Their youngest daughter, Jessie Rinn, recalled much of the story.[2]

How I Met Lewis Rinn

Told in the imagined words of Marguerite Clair

"I turned nineteen in the summer of 1876 and my life changed forever.

Just a few months previously, Papa came to me and said, "Maggie, you need to improve your English. You need to get away from Silkville."

You see, I was twelve when we left our beloved France and came to Kansas where Papa helped to establish the silk weaving commune near Williamsburg, Kansas. People came from all over the world, but most of the people we knew best were from France. Mama didn't learn English so we spoke French at home.

Papa said, "Our friends, the Hurets from Silkville, run a boarding house at Camp Supply. They need a cook for the summer. Mama taught you to be a good cook and I think you should go down there. It will be a chance for you to use your English and it will only be for the summer."

How could Papa expect me to leave my family and go off by myself more than 300 miles into Indian (Oklahoma) Territory to an army camp that was on the frontier? Weren't there only soldiers, cowboys, and Indians there? Papa said I would be safe with his friends. The more I thought about it, the more exciting it sounded. I liked to have fun, and this would be quite an adventure.

So off to Camp Supply I went. My first impression of Camp Supply was disappointing. It was a bleak army fort located in the northwest part of Indian Territory far from any town. The boarding house was outside the fort and various boarders who had business with the army rented rooms. I set to work getting settled and getting busy in the kitchen. I loved to cook and my food was good.

At first, I was timid and shy around the boarders. Soon, I got to know them and became my usual self. We all loved to laugh and joke. The men took an interest in me. I guess they thought I was cute with my French accent, and I was petite, being less than five feet tall, with dark hair and eyes.

One of the boarders, Lewis Rinn, a 35-year-old butcher [he mistakenly thought he was 34], took a special interest in me. I thought he was so good looking with his thick, dark hair and blue eyes. He had been a Union army soldier during the war and had come to America from Germany with his family when he was 10 years-old. He said he would be happy to help me improve my English. I wasn't too sure how my English would be better considering his German accent, but I liked spending time with Lewis. Before long we were inseparable.

Lewis was a confirmed bachelor, but seemed taken by me. He wanted to do everything for me. Oh, I was smitten too. I felt adored and knew that no one would ever love me more. Lewis asked me to marry him and declared that he wanted to have a family and take care of me for the rest of his life. This was so romantic for me. My birthday was on July 29, so Lewis whisked me off to Dodge City, Kansas, to be married on my birthday. We traveled the 100 miles to Dodge City, found a justice of the peace and were married on my nineteenth birthday, Saturday, July 29, 1876."

Early Dodge City

Front Street, Dodge City, Kansas 1867 (Dodge City and Ford County)

When Lewis and Marguerite went to Dodge City, Kansas, to be married, they found a wide-open frontier town described as a lawless town:

> It sprang out of a barrel of whiskey. For 10 years it thrived on whiskey, and city politics revolved around whiskey. The "Wickedest Little City in America" became its nickname. The Atchison, Topeka & Santa Fe Railroad was laying track toward Fort Dodge, bringing hundreds of workers. By the time the tracks arrived in September 1872, several businesses had been established, some still in tents.
>
> Dodge City wasn't incorporated until November 1875, and Ford County wasn't organized until 1873, so for its first year, there was no law or official government in Dodge. Boot Hill, though, was firmly established.
>
> Dodge immediately became a major shipping point for buffalo hunters. By 1873 some 2,000 hunters roamed western Kansas. In a three-year period, 850,000 hides were shipped east out of Dodge, 754,529 of those in 1873. That same year, millions of pounds of buffalo meat and 50 carloads of buffalo tongues were also shipped out.

By 1875 the buffalo was virtually gone from the area, but there was another animal waiting to take its place, the Texas Longhorn. The cowboy replaced the buffalo hunter in Dodge City. Some of the hunters stayed around, though, and went into the saloon business as owners, part-owners, bartenders, or gamblers. Others became lawmen. Several did both. In 1877, with a population of less than 1,000, Dodge had 16 saloons, plus dance halls and brothels. The saloons changed ownership partners and locations so often one almost needed a scorecard to keep track of all the players.

The early city government and law enforcement were controlled by the Dodge City Gang, a group of merchants, saloonkeepers, and gamblers in favor of a wide-open town to accommodate the Texas cowboy.[3]

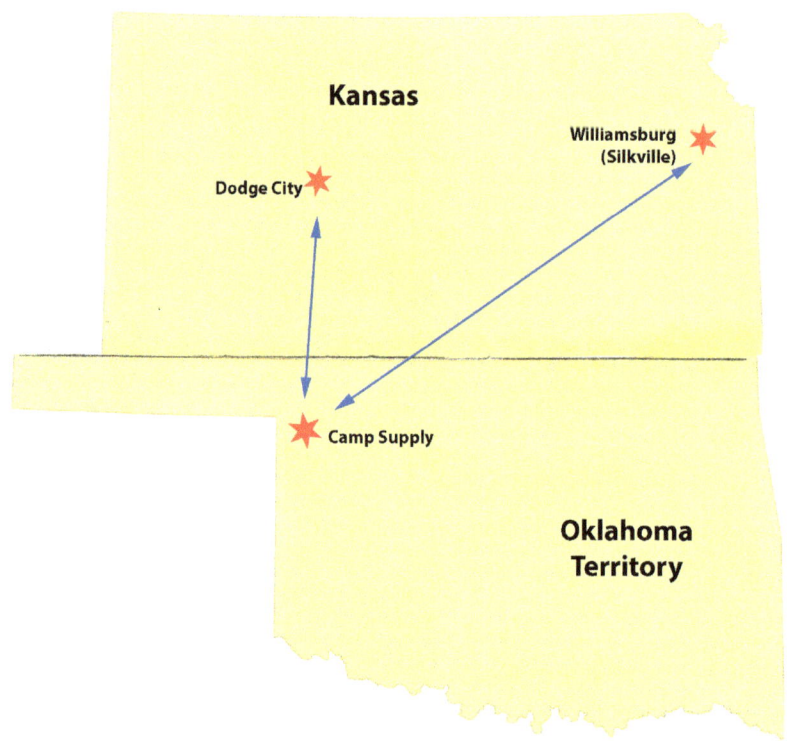

Camp Supply to Dodge City, Kansas 100 miles
Camp Supply to Silkville, Kansas 300 miles

Chapter 2

LIVING AT CAMP SUPPLY
1876-1883

The couple returned to Camp Supply to establish a home for the next six years. It is not known when Marguerite's parents were told about the marriage, nor what they thought about their young daughter marrying an older German. As a wedding gift, the Clairs had an elaborate bedspread made in their native Saint Etienne, France, to be given to the couple. It took a year to be completed and remains in the family as a keepsake.[4]

*Handmade bedspread, a wedding gift from Claude and Benoite Clair.
In possession of Bill Thompson (2004).*

Challenges of Living on the Frontier

Life must have been challenging for Marguerite, newly married, young and away from family. On May 30, 1877, just 10 months after her marriage, Lottie was born on May, 30, 1877, followed by Claire on December 2, 1879, and Daniel Claude on October 1, 1881—three children in four years.[5] Lewis had to leave Marguerite and baby Lottie to travel to Fort Smith, Arkansas, in July 1878 to serve as a witness to a murder that had taken place on the army post.[6]

> Mr. Lewis Rinn, post butcher of Camp Supply, I. T., passed through Dodge, Tuesday, on his way to Fort Smith, to which place he has been summoned as a witness in a murder case, against George Thomas, colored, who killed one Gibbs; also a colored man last April, at Camp Supply.

Dodge City Globe Newspaper-July 9, 1878

Fort Supply, Indian Territory-Frontier Outpost on the Plains

Camp Supply's name was changed to Fort Supply. Lewis Rinn likely made good money as the army post butcher, but they lived a true pioneer experience as described by Robert Carriker:

> Fort Supply, originally known as Camp Supply, was located in the far western Cherokee Outlet in present-day Woodward County, Oklahoma. The military post was established in November 1868 as a base of operations for a winter campaign against the Kiowa, Comanche, and Cheyenne Indian tribes.
>
> Indian Territory during the last three decades of the nineteenth century was described as a nether world of whiskey merchants, cattle and timber thieves, speculators, tribal opportunists, and various other frontier thugs.
>
> Life at Fort Supply, deep within Indian Territory, was a true pioneer experience. As the settlement attracted a civilian population, social life flourished. Water, ice, and fresh vegetables at Fort Supply were both necessities and luxuries. None were easy to come by, but ingenuity and persistence made them available by one means or another.

The weather in northwest Indian Territory did not make life more pleasant, or less exciting. In July and August temperatures regularly ranged around the 100-degree mark, and from November to March a sudden blue northerner could bring a rapid drop in temperature. Winds were constant, from the south in summer, from the north in winter.

Supplies came to the community from Fort Dodge, Kansas, via the Dodge-Supply road. After 1878, mail from Dodge City to Fort Supply was delivered twice each week. Originally, there was just one trading store, but by the close of the 1870's, there were other businessmen at Fort Supply, and many stores had opened on Washington Ave. Tailors advertised "genuine Parisian style," and boot makers, barbers, and dry-goods merchants offered good wares and services at reasonable prices.

Evening amusements included strolling shows, magicians, road companies, and band concerts. The arrival of the regimental band at the army post offered the best entertainment for the community. They usually spent two or three weeks each year performing concerts and dances. Holidays were special occasions. Christmas was pleasant, but the "real" holiday was the Fourth of July. Usually, a baseball game started the festivities, followed by foot, sack, and wheelbarrow races. In the last contest of the day, entrants tried to catch a greased pig. Music and dancing out-of-doors closed the program.[7]

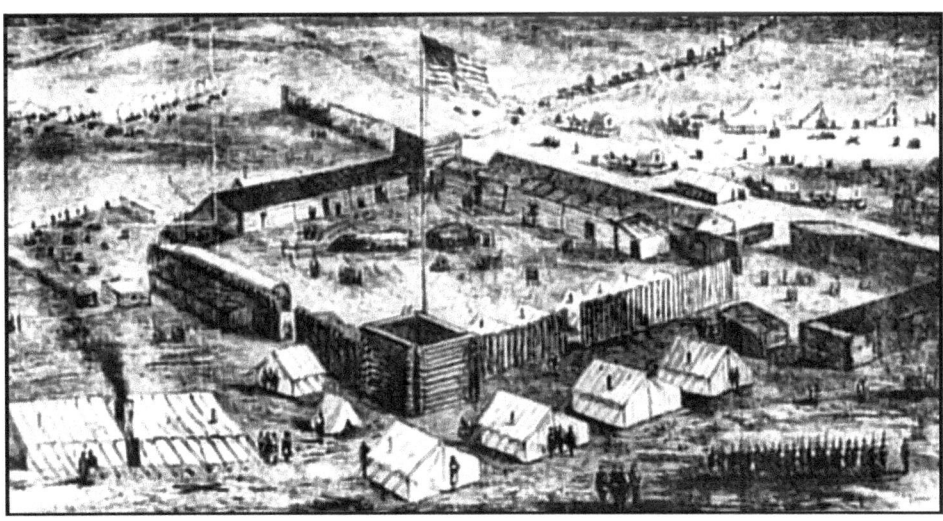

Camp Supply, Indian Territory, 1869, Rinns lived outside post
(Fort Supply, Indian Territory by Carriker)

Lewis Shopped at Tiffany's February 1881

From time to time, Lewis Rinn took cattle east. Apparently, he was very successful in 1881 because on February 14, 1881, he purchased a gold watch at Tiffany's in New York City for $128, which is $3393 in 2020 money.[8] The watch and receipt is held in Edmond Rinn's family artifacts. It is not known if Marguerite was with him.

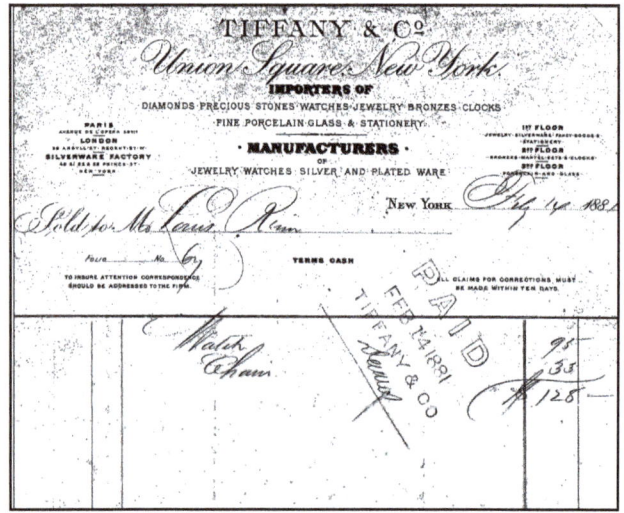

Receipt for watch

Expensive gold pocket-watch, Purchased by Lewis Rinn, In New York City. (photo by Janelle Richardson 2009)

Marguerite's Father Died

In the summer of 1881, Marguerite's father, Claude Clair, went to Saint Louis to seek medical treatment for his failing health.[9] Soon after returning to Silkville, he conducted a sale of his household goods and sent a trunk to Fort Supply.[10] Hoping to return to France, Claude Clair died in New York City on December 1, 1881.[11]

Disaster When Family Traveled East Later

Youngest daughter, Jessie Rinn, said in a taped interview, that she heard that her folks traveled east when they had three small children, which would be after the birth of Daniel Claude Rinn in October 1881.[12] She thought they went to Pennsylvania. But the family may have gone to New York City to be with Marguerite's mother, Benoite Clair when Claude Clair died. However,

Daniel Claude Rinn was only two months old and it was likely too soon for Marguerite to travel. The family story was that when the family returned home to Fort Supply, they found their house destroyed by fire. The hired man had left a candle burning. They lost almost everything except the clothing in their travel trunks.[13]

 The couple started all over and remained at Camp Supply for a short time. Marguerite's mother and sister, Benoite and Theodie Clair, lived there with them too. Years later, Leota Jardon Hunt would write that her mother, Theodie Clair, said they lived for a while down in Indian Territory with the Rinns.[14] By February 1883, the Rinns relocated to Williamsburg, Kansas, where Violet Rinn was born.[15]

Chapter 3

MOVING TO KANSAS
1882-1901

Remains of Clair house where Rinns likely lived 1883-1887.
(Photo by Janelle Richardson (1997)

Lived at Silkville

The Lewis Rinn family left Fort Supply and moved to the Clair place at Silkville, Kansas, late in 1882.[16] Several factors likely influenced their move. Marguerite's father, Claude Clair, died in 1881 leaving her mother and sister in Kansas.[17] Diminished fort population may have made it less profitable for Lewis to sell meat to the army. Frontier life no longer met the needs of the growing family with school-aged children. The Rinns left Fort Supply, traveled with three small children 300 plus miles to Silkville. In July 1883, Lewis Rinn bought the 160 acres from E. V. Broissier that had been the original site where the Claude Clair family lived at Silkville. It was the NE quarter of Section 2, Township 19, Range 17 East, of Franklin County, Kansas. Rinn bought the land for $1,920 with a mortgage given by Broissier.[18] Rinn may have signed a contract with his mother-in-law, Benoite Clair, for the improvements on the land.[19]

Family Grew

Soon after the couple relocated, Violet Rinn was born February 25, 1883. Theoda Rinn was born February 22, 1885, and Lewis Rinn born December 26, 1887.[20] Lewis Rinn was listed on the 1885 Kansas State Census as a farmer with Benoite and Theodie Clair living with the Rinn family.[21] The local newspaper reported the Rinns hosting a dance.

A festive hop is reported at the house of Lewis Rinn, Saturday night, in which several couple from town participated.

Dance held at Rinn home (Independent Journal, Ottawa Kansas Newspaper, p.2, April 26, 1883)

Ten Thousand Dollar Mystery

Lewis Rinn made a deposit of $10,300 in the Ottawa, Kansas bank in 1882. This would be worth approximately $265,000 in 2020.[22] The mystery is, where did the money come from, and where did it go? According to Kansas deed records, the Rinns always had a mortgage on their property.

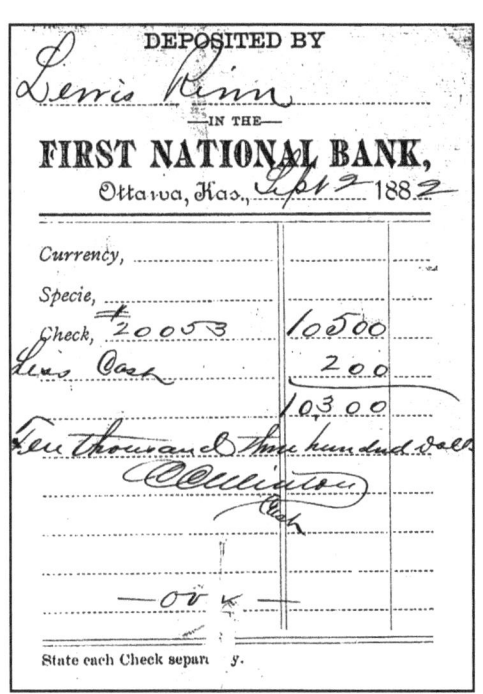

Bank Deposit for $10,300, (Held in Jessie Rinn family artifacts)

Photos Show Stylish Couple

As a 45-year-old confident farmer/businessman, blue-eyed Lewis Rinn wore his brown hair cut short and a mustahe anchored his prominent nose. He wore a business suit, white shirt, and ribbon bow tie, likely fashioned from silk ribbons from Silkville. His younger wife, Marguerite, wore a dark dress accented by a large ribbon scarf, also likely from Silkville ribbon. Her dark hair formed small pincurls that framed her face with her remaining hair pulled back and on top of her head.

Marguerite Rinn,
(late 1880s-about 30 years old)

Lewis Rinn,
(late 1880s-about 45 years old)

Lewis Rinn Bred Animals

Likely Lewis Rinn did not have a meat market initially in Kansas. Instead he was a breeder of championship cattle, hogs, and thoroughbred horses. In 1885, he was listed in the American Berkshire Record owning bulls "Young Carlisle" and "Plantagenet." The American Short-Horn Herd book in 1889 noted him as the breeder of "Ella P," a champion calf.[23] A series of announcements in the Williamsburg and Ottawa newspapers beginning in 1883 describe his activities.

> Mr. Lewis Rinn, of Williamsburg, was in the city on Tuesday, with his fine thoroughbred colt "Fred Sprague." Of course he stayed over to see the "spotted" elephant in the evening, not seeing him in the parade in the morning.

Lewis Rinn & Colt "Fred Sprague",
(Ottawa Weekly Republic, Ottawa, Kansas Newspaper, p. 4 Oct 25, 1883)

> If any of our farmers wants to see a couple of equine beauties, let them take a look at Lewis Rinn's spring colts—both sired by his stallion.

Lewis Rinn's Colts,
(Ottawa Daily News, Ottawa, Kansas Newspaper, p.1, Aug 26, 1887)

House Burned

Late in March 1887, a fire took place at the Rinn house. The frame of the stone building remained intact, but everything else was destroyed. Likely the fire prompted the family to move into the nearby town of Williamsburg. In February 1888, Lewis Rinn sold the Silkville property back to E. V. Broissier including the acreage and improvements for $2,358.[24] (worth about $67,190 in 2020).[25]

> —Lewis Rinn, of Willirmsburg tp. lost his residence by fire. No insurance. Loss, $1,500.

Rinn House Lost 1887
(Independent Journal, Ottawa, Kansas Newspaper p.2 Mar 31, 1887)

Sister Theodie Clair Married

At the age of 18, Marguerite's sister, Theodie Clair married Martin Jardon on April 25, 1888.[26] The Jardon family originated in France. The young couple made their home near Baldwin City, in nearby Douglas County, Kansas. Benoite Clair likely lived with them.

Lived in Town of Williamsburg 1887-1901

The Rinn family lived in the town of Williamsburg, which had a population of about 400 people in the early 1880s. William Cutler, in his book, *History of the State of Kansas*, described Williamsburg in the early 1880s this way:

> This enterprising town is in Williamsburg Township, in the southwest corner of the Franklin County. Attracted by the abundance of excellent coal in that part of the county, a number of parties purchased land in 1867. Quite a number of permanent settlements were made in 1868.
>
> Dr. Aitken opened a drug and grocery store in 1870, and John Boston who arrived in Williamsburg, April 2, 1870, started a wagon shop that year. Lott Wainwright started a blacksmith shop in 1869. The school district, No. 51, was organized July 16, 1868, and the schoolhouse was built in the summer of 1870. The first school was taught the following winter.
>
> At the present time Williamsburg contains four general stores, one hardware, one grocery and two drug stores, one harness, two blacksmith, two wagon and two boot and shoe shops, two agricultural implement dealers, three lumber yards, three physicians, one newspaper, and has about 400 inhabitants. It has one newspaper, *The Weekly Gazette*, established April 3, 1880, by Frank Bennett. This is a four-column folio, devoted to local interests, and neutral in politics.[27]

Downtown Williamsburg, about 1900, Rinn Meat Market Located Across Street
(Williamsburg Museum photo)

Remaining Rinn Children Born

Edward was born in 1889, Edmond was born July 29, 1891, Seona was born September 10, 1893, and Jessie was born January1,1896,[28] completing the family of six girls and four boys born over a period of 19 years. Edward died young, believed to have taken sick from eating candy. The older Rinn children went to school in Williamsburg. There is no record, but it appears they probably completed the eighth grade or higher. At home, they were taught the value of hard work. If they tried hard enough, they could achieve. Marguerite taught her girls to be good homemakers–excellent seamstresses and outstanding cooks. No doubt, they all helped in the butcher and ice cream shops. The girls competed to see who could meet their Dad at the door and give him his pipe and slippers when he came home.

Williamsburg School Rinn Children Attended (Williamsburg Museum photo)

Marguerite Received Small Inheritance in 1889

It took several years for the family to settle the estate of Claude Clair, who passed away in 1881. Marguerite's younger brother, Pierre "Peter," left home and went to Colorado in 1880. At first, the family heard from him, thereafter they had no word from him. Eventually, he was declared dead. There was a dispute between Lewis Rinn and his mother-in-law, Benoite Clair. Lewis went to the court and filed an affidavit stating that Benoite Clair had never filed an inventory for the estate and that he felt that $1,600 had not been accounted for. Immediately, in February 1888, Benoite Clair hired a lawyer and answered the claim, denying that she was withholding $1,600. In fact, she claimed that Lewis Rinn had defaulted on his contract with her to buy her house and buildings on the Silkville property. He had paid only $267 on the $2,500 contract.[29] The dispute was resolved, and the estate was finally settled on April 22, 1889. Marguerite Clair Rinn received $195.26 as her part of the estate-which would be the equivalent of $3,700 in current dollars.[30]

Ran Meat Market and Ice Cream Store

In 1895, Lewis opened a meat market on Williams Street in Williamsburg. Lewis ran the meat market, and by 1898 Marguerite ran a seasonal ice cream shop next door.[31] The family may have lived a couple blocks north on Main Ave. as the local newspaper reported in 1900 that they painted their house located on Main.[32] The busy parents often took their younger children with them into the shops. One night, ready to sit down to supper, the Rinns missed one of the children. Hurrying back to the shop, they found a very frightened Edmond, who had been asleep under the counter.[33]

Unlike most women in Williamsburg, Marguerite, the mother of nine children, ran her business and owned the business lot.[34] At the time of this ad, Jessie her youngest, was two years old. How did she manage? Her oldest daughters likely helped at home. Years later, Jessie recalled that her sister, Violet, was like a second mother.[35]

Where Rinn Meat Market and Ice Cream Shop Once Stood
(Photo taken 2003 by Janelle Richardson)

> **HAVING RENTED THE**
> # MEAT MARKET
> in the Burg, we wish to notify the p cpl that we will keep constantly on hand the best meat the market will afford.
> We solicit your patronage.
> YOURS TO PLEASE.
> ## LEWIS RINN.

Williamsburg Star, August 1895,

> Beers and McCurdy have leased their meat market to Lewis Rinn for one year from May 1st. Mr. Rinn is a practical butcher and we wish him success in the business.

Williamsburg Star, April 1895

> **We are together, yet we are separate.**
>
> | On the left hand side is.... | On the right hand side is.... |
> |---|---|
> | MRS. RINN'S | LEWIS RINN'S |
> | Confectionery, Ice Cream, and General Refreshment Stand. | Meat Market, with a full stock of finely selected fresh meats. |
>
> We vie with each other in our efforts to please.

Williamsburg Star, September 1898

Family Visited Ottawa, Kansas

Williamsburg was a very small town, but Ottawa, with a population of 5,000 people and many stores was just 15 miles away. Two trains a day stopped at Williamsburg headed for Ottawa. Ottawa, in 1875, had three fine halls, one court-room, four large hardware stores, two stove and tin shops, eleven dry goods, twenty groceries, three clothing stores, three boots and shoes stores, two book stores, one drug store, four millinery, three jewelry, four confectionery and bakery establishments, five stables, seven hotels, one billiard saloon, half a dozen eating houses, three extensive lumber yards, and so forth. It supported 11 lawyers, as many doctors, four dentists, a score of real estate and insurance men, one private banker, and some street brokers.[36]

20th Century Began

The twentieth century began on a Tuesday, and Lewis and Marguerite Rinn and their nine children were living in Williamsburg, Kansas. Their children ranged in age from four-year-old Jessie, to twenty-three-year old Lottie. Lewis told the census taker, George Launders, on June 7, 1900, that he was 58 and wife Marguerite was 42.

The 1900 census lists Lewis as a butcher who owned a home with a mortgage. He said he was born in Germany and immigrated in 1852, although it was actually October 1851 when he arrived. He said he was naturalized. Marguerite said she was born in France and came to the United States in 1869. She was not naturalized–this was prior to women having the vote. She did not list a job, although she ran an ice cream shop, and sold specialized food, working much of the time. Both parents said they could read and write.

Lottie, Claire, and Daniel C. were listed as being born in Indian Territory. Lottie was 23 and worked as a servant in the L.C. Stine home in Ottawa. Claire did not list a job, and 18-year-old Daniel, who the family called Claude, was listed as attending school four months that year. All the rest of the children were listed as being born in Kansas and attending school, with the exception of Jessie, who was still too young for school.[37]

Life In Williamsburg

We do not know all the details of family life for the Rinns, but short items from the Williamsburg Newspapers for 1893-1901 reveal some information. Williamsburg began to grow and prosper. In October, 1893, the newspaper reported, "*There are no vacant business houses or offices in town, and but very few if any vacant residences. Business is good and houses are in demand.*" By 1901, the town had grown to 700 people and the paper reported, "*Saturday, no less than 200 teams and vehicles of various kinds were in town, and the stores were crowded with buyers and the clerks were kept on the jump. Saturday is the one great trading day for the country folk. The fact is well known that Williamsburg is once again coming toward the head of the list, where it used to be for so long as the country's trading point for 20 miles around."*[38]

The Rinns were busy with their shops. The newspaper reported in November 1897 that *"Mrs. Rinn is prepared to serve fresh oysters; or will sell them by the can."* In April 1900, the family made improvements on their residence and put a new counter and soda fountain in their business. Then in October of that year the outside of the business front was painted red. The Rinns had a telephone installed at their business in December 1900. They had one of the 120 phones in town and their telephone number was 60.

Built Ice House

Lewis Rinn had a large ice house probably located behind his store and maybe underground. During the winter, ice blocks from nearby freshwater sources were cut into squares and brought in and stored there. Materials such as sawdust or straw covered the ice, thus providing effective insulation. This method could store ice as long as into the early to mid-summertime. The December 1898 newspaper reported that, *"Lewis Rinn is filling his ice house with nice eight-inch ice from the pond in the north east part of town."* Other years, ice was not available until later. The December 21, 1900 newspaper said, *"Lewis Rinn is securing sawdust for his ice house. But up to this writing, no ice has appeared."* Then in February 15, 1901 it was reported that, *"Mr. Lewis Rinn yesterday finished filling his large ice house. It looks now as though we might be pretty well supplied with ice through the coming season."*[39]

> Lewis Rinn is filling his ice house with nice eight inch ice from the pond in north east part of town.

Williamsburg Star, December 16, 1898

> Lewis Rinn is erecting a stone slaughter house on the lots west of the old slaughter house.

Williamsburg Star, May 2, 1896

Cutting and hauling ice, 1890s ice house

Special Town Activities

Williamsburg often had special activities. The circus, Labor Day, Fourth of July, and band performances were big celebrations. Lottie, the oldest daughter, working in Ottawa, came home for the fair.[40]

Rinn's Visited Family and Friends

As reported in the newspapers, the Rinns frequently traveled by train the 30 miles to Baldwin, Kansas, to visit Marguerite's mother, Benoite Clair, and her sister's family, the Jardons.

These relatives frequently visited Williamsburg. Old friends from the days of Marguerite growing up in Silkville, Mr. and Mrs. Julius Lachiene, visited often.[41]

Rinns Active Members of Knights and Ladies of Security

The family was active in the Knights and Ladies of Security which met on Wednesday evening twice a month. This was a social and benevolent society. Following the Civil War, fraternal benefit orders became popular as a means of providing financial protection or insurance for its members' widows and orphans at affordable prices. Many orders also had lodges where members met to socialize. Secret ritual ceremonies and regalia such as pins, swords and flags were part of the organizations.

Knights and Ladies of Security Pin

In 1889 Lewis and Marguerite traveled the 80 miles to Leavenworth, Kansas, to attend a meeting. They likely went by train and may have taken the family.

The Select Knights was the Ancient Order of United Workmen (AOUW) which was founded in 1868. Originally, members paid $1 into the insurance fund to cover a death benefit. Each time a member died, $1 was due from the surviving members to reestablish the fund. By 1887, the order had 176,000 members across the county. In the 1940s the order had been absorbed into the Pioneer Mutual Life Insurance Company which was taken over by American United Life Insurance Company and is now part of OneAmerica.[42]

The Knights and Ladies of Security was a fraternal and benevolent society founded in 1892 in Kansas. Soon it had 238 local lodges in Kansas, Nebraska, Iowa and Missouri. By 1911 the order had spread to 30 states having a total membership of about 120,000 and had disbursed about $7,500,000 in benefits. In 1919 it changed its name to The Security Benefit Association and in 1950 to Security Benefit Life Insurance Company and is still active.[43]

As the Rinn children reached adulthood, they became members of the Knights and Ladies of Security in Williamsburg. The local newspaper reported Clair and Daniel Rinn joining.[44]

> Mr. and Mrs. Lewis Rinn attended the K. of P. meeting of the grand lodge at Leavenworth this week.

Announcement Williamsburg Star May 30, 1889

Williamsburg, Kansas, had active AOUW and Knights and Ladies of Security lodges. The local newspaper stated on January 26, 1900:

> The AOUW in this place at their last meeting initiated four new members and reinstalled a number and there are several more ready to ride the goat at their next meeting.
>
> The Knights and Ladies of Security at their last regular meeting initiated two new members and are to initiate six beneficiary members at their next meeting. After initiation last Wednesday evening the geographical party, given by Mrs. McMillan, was reported to be a grand success and contributed greatly to the enjoyment of all present. This order is greatly growing in strength and number. The program for social entertainment for each regular meeting keeps a pleasant evening always in anticipation for the members.

Lewis Rinn Suffered from Rheumatism

From time to time Lewis Rinn suffered from poor health. As early as July 1896, at the age of 55, he made claim to be placed on the Disability Pension Roll for Civil War Veterans. He said he was unable to do physical labor due to rheumatism and associated weakened kidneys.[45] The September 8, 1899 newspaper reported that, *"Mr. Rinn has been quite sick."* Then on September 22, they reported that, *"Mr. Lewis Rinn is getting about again this week after a severe attack of rheumatism."*[46]

Lewis Rinn Won Land in Oklahoma

1901 Land lottery, El Reno, Oklahoma where Lewis Rinn went to register for land

Land openings in Oklahoma Territory beginning in 1889 brought much excitement and talk in Kansas. Under the Homestead Act, people could stake out a claim for 160 acres. Much of the land was said to be good farming land. The early land openings were held with land runs where applicants lined up at a starting point and ran for their desired land. This method resulted in many accidents, disappointments, injustices, heartbreaks, and homicides. Congress learned that they needed a better method than a horse race to distribute the homesteads of Oklahoma's valuable territory. The government decided in 1901 that the last great land opening would be parceled out by lottery. More than 160,000 people congregated in El Reno, beginning on July 9, 1901, to sign up for land during a 30-day period.[47] Lewis Rinn had a friend in Williamsburg who was excited about the possibility of getting land. He talked Lewis into going down to El Reno with him to apply. The local newspaper reported on July 20, 1901 that Lewis Rinn was in El Reno for the big land drawing. A round trip ticket from Williamsburg to El Reno cost $12.39. About 500 men from Franklin County made the trip.[48]

Every train arriving in El Reno was loaded with land seekers. The town, with a normal population of about 7,000 people, was swamped. The hotels and restaurants were soon full, and the visitors erected tents and booths much like a street carnival. Fortunately, during the 30 days, the weather was fair and suitable for outdoor living. A better-humored or more orderly crowd could not have been congregated anywhere. As the people waited, they organized their own entertainment; they organized by states, they gave parades, held church services, lectures, and concerts. Saloons and gambling houses were open, but there was comparatively little excessive drinking and practically no disorder.[49]

Applicants such as Lewis Rinn had an opportunity to learn about the available lands to be drawn. Vendors sold maps. Locators took hack-loads of people into the new country to look over the land so they might know what the preferred sections were. Lewis probably had a chance to look over his preferred land southwest of El Reno. There were 25 registration booths where Lewis and his friend stood in line to register. Their registration certificates were placed in sealed envelopes and put in one of two large lottery wheels that were about six feet long and four feet in diameter. Many applicants reported standing in line from 8 in the morning to 3:30 o'clock. The actual drawing took place on July 29, 1901, at 9 a.m. at El Reno. There were 10 applicants for every parcel of land. Ten names were drawn at a time. They were opened, read, and filed, and then the list of names was given for publication.

Family tradition says that Lewis returned to Kansas awaiting results of the lottery. His friend did not get land, but he was one of the lucky winners with drawing a low number to get his choice of land.[50] One day, the postman came running down the streets of Williamsburg carrying a post card shouting, *"Rinn drew land. Rinn drew land in Oklahoma."* [51]

Rinns Prepared to Leave Kansas

To qualify to homestead the land, the Rinns needed to occupy the land within 90 days. The family set about preparing to leave Kansas. Lewis Rinn made at least two trips back to Oklahoma in August and September 1901. The local newspaper reported on August 17th that he returned from El Reno on Tuesday morning.[52] Likely he went to file for his homestead on August 10th, for Section 18, Township 10N, Range 8 West.[53] The newspaper reported on Sept 7th that Lewis Rinn went to Oklahoma on Tuesday and then reported on Sept 14th that he returned from El Reno on Tuesday morning.[54] He may have made arrangements to start construction of a log cabin to house his family.

The three oldest Rinn children, Lottie, Claire, and Daniel Claude, stayed in Kansas. Daniel Hare purchased the Williamsburg meat market. The newspaper reported on November 2, 1901 that Dan Rinn assisted in the Northside Meat Market.[55]

Ad appearing in Williamsburg newspaper, October 1901 with new owner of meat market.

The family butchered and cured meat, and loaded two or three covered wagons with supplies. The family, consisting of six children aged 5 to 18, and the help of two hired men to drive the covered wagons, set out for Oklahoma on October 29, 1901.[56] Daughters Violet and Theoda rode their father's two beloved racehorses. Family tradition says that the family was very sad to leave Williamsburg. The streets were lined with well-wishers, and many a tear was shed.[57]

Why Did the Rinns Leave Kansas to Homestead in Oklahoma?

The Rinns left the security of living in an established Kansas town where they had been for 18 years and ran a successful butcher shop. Why did they venture into the unsettled Oklahoma Territory? At first, they lived in the wilderness with limited supplies, no source of income, and lots of work to be done. Lewis was 60 years old and in poor health. His thinking is not known, but possibly he wanted his family to have a farm that could support them after he was gone.

Chapter 4

BREAKING THE SOD IN OKLAHOMA

We're Home

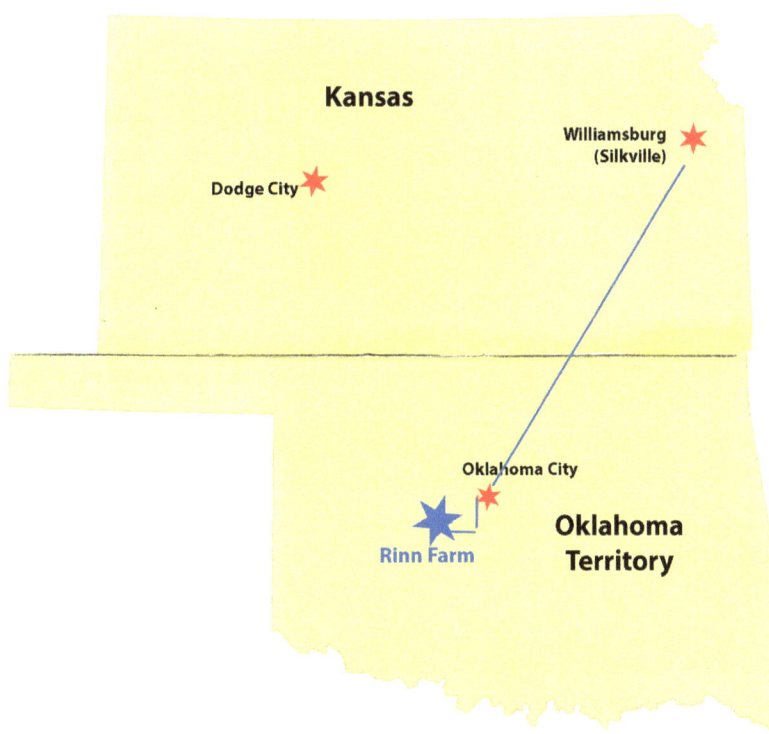

Rinns Traveled by Covered Wagon to Oklahoma

On November 17, 1901, the weary Rinn family had traveled more than 300 miles by covered wagon for three weeks south thru Kansas and west across Oklahoma. Lewis Rinn halted the wagons, took off his hat, exposing his thick gray hair, and said, "We're home." They had arrived at their homestead 11 miles northwest of the town of Minco, Grady County. The younger children, Lewis Jr., Edmond, Seona and Jessie tumbled out of the wagons, joined hands, jumped up and down, and screamed with excitement. They loved this land with its slopping hills and meandering creek.[58] The family erected two tents for the boys to sleep in. The girls slept in the wagons until a three-room house with a solid roof could be finished before the onset of winter.[59] The Williamsburg newspaper reported their arrival, and son, Daniel Claude Rinn, transported the family furnishings and livestock by train, likely to the train station at El Reno or Minco.[60]

It is not hard to imagine the hardships the family endured the first winter. Winter came early with a subzero temperature of 2 degrees below zero recorded on December 14 in Oklahoma City.[61] Since Lewis Rinn suffered from rheumatism and stomach troubles, son Daniel Claude, and their hired hands, Will Marrow and another worker, built the house and cleared the land.[62] But there were many friendly Indians in the area, as well as wild goats, turkeys, bobcats, and wild, long-horned steers roaming around.

Opening Meat Market Minco

While still in Kansas, Lewis Rinn said he planned to open a meat market in Minco, Oklahoma, which was one mile south and ten miles east of his homestead. Likely he needed to generate income.[63] He ran an ad in the *Minco Minstrel* newspaper on March 21, 1902. His business, City Meat Market, was on East Main Street, Minco, Indian Territory. It is not known who Henry, the co-proprietor was.[64] Lewis and Marguerite may have stayed in town part of the time while daughters, 18-year-old Violet, and 16-year-old Theoda, kept house at the homestead.[65] Lewis did not keep the shop in Minco very long. There was only one advertisement from 1902-1903 in the newspaper. Thereafter, the butcher shop appeared to be owned

Ad for Lewis Rinn's Meat Market, March 1902, Minco Minstrel

by someone else. Lewis Rinn may have been physically unable to run a meat market or he may have found traveling between his homestead and Minco difficult. Roads were crude and Buggy Creek, a creek near his homestead, often swelled so much after a rain that it was impossible to get to Minco.

By spring 1902, older daughters, Lottie and Clair, joined the family. They found work in El Reno, about 30 miles away. They lived there with frequent visits home. Lottie worked for Singer Sewing Machine.[66] By that time, the 14-by-48-foot log house (672 square feet) with three to four rooms had been built. A crop was planted on 40 acres. Work progressed on digging a well, planting a fruit orchard, fencing the pasture, and building a barn and hen house.[67] Everything was going well until the summer of 1902.

Rinn Homestead Almost Lost

AS IMAGINED IN THE WORDS OF LEWIS RINN STORY BASED ON LAND PATENT FILE 544[68]

"It was a warm July morning in 1902 on our Rinn Homestead in Oklahoma Territory. Work began early because there was much to do to establish a productive farm on uncultivated land that once belonged to the Indians. Everyone worked hard, but it was worth it because the land would soon belong to us. I had been lucky when I left home in Kansas and came to the territory in the summer of 1901 and selected land for the lottery. Later that summer, almost everyone in our small town of Williamsburg, Kansas, heard the postman come down Main Street waving a postcard and shouting, "Rinn won land, Rinn won land."

Out of over 160,000 applicants, I was one of the lucky 13,000 who drew land. I believed that my selection would be good farmland. Once I completed the requirements for homesteading, the 160 acres would be mine.

But later that July, an official government letter addressed to Mr. Lewis Rinn, arrived in the weekly mail. I couldn't believe what I read. Everyone could hear me swear, "What the hell are they trying to do to me?" The letter said I had sixty days to prove that I was a citizen of the United States, or I would lose my claim.

When I filled out my Homestead Entry Paper on August 10, 1901, I stated that I came to the United States with my parents as a young boy, ten years old, from Germany. My father, Ludwig Rinn, was a naturalized citizen, which makes me a citizen. How dare the government ask me for proof that my father became a citizen. I have no proof. My father died many years ago in Pennsylvania. Did the government expect me to carry his naturalization papers around with me for more than 40 years? Here is the letter I received:

> July 12, 1902
>
> Lewis Rinn   Evidence of naturalization or statement of military service required.
> Register and Receiver
>
> El Reno, O.T.
>
> Gentlemen:
>
> Lewis Rinn of Williamsburg, Kansas, who made H.E. #544, El Reno, August 10, 1901, for the NE ¼ Sec. 18, T. 10N., R. 8 W., alleged in his homestead affidavit that he came to this country when a child, but that his father became a naturalized citizen before the applicant came of age, but he furnishes no evidence of his father's alleged naturalization. He also states that he is an honorably discharged soldier of the war of the rebellion, but gives no data of the services thus rendered.
>
> You will accordingly notify him that he will be allowed sixty days from notice within which to furnish a certified copy of his father's certificate of naturalization or other sufficient evidence of same, or to furnish in lieu thereof a certified copy of his discharge or such other evidence of his military service offered as will enable this office to have some verified from the records of the War Department, advising him at the same time that in the event of his failure to respond hereto or appeal here from, his said entry, hereby held for cancellation, will be canceled without further notice to him from this office.
>
>> Serve notice and make report in accordance with circuit law of March 1, 1900. (29 L.D., 649).
>>
>> Very respectfully,
>>
>> Assistant Commissioner

My beloved wife, Marguerite, responded to the news in her excitable French manner. She cried. In her French accent she said, "We can't lose this place. We have sacrificed too much. We can't go back. We already sold everything in Kansas."

I decided I am not going to let the government take my homestead. This is my country, and I deserve the land. Wasn't I the one who answered President Lincoln's call for volunteers when I proudly stood in line in Pittsburgh on July 4, 1861, as a 21-year-old recruit for the Union Army? I served my country for three years in Pennsylvania's 62nd Regiment during the Civil War. I am proud of surviving the many battles, as I served in the Army of the Potomac. Even now, at the age of 60, I am an active member of the Grand Army of the Republic, the veteran's group of the Union Army.

I saddled my horse and rode into the town of Minco 11 miles away to speak with an attorney. He helped me respond to the government letter by stating that I couldn't furnish proof of my father's citizenship, but I had a right to the Homestead because I was eligible for immediate citizenship based on my service as a Union Army soldier during the Civil War. We set in motion the process of getting a certified copy of my discharge papers. The government responded and agreed that I could qualify for naturalization and be able to get my homestead and become a citizen both at the same time.

To prove or get title to my land, I needed to pay $1.25 per acre which amounted to $200. Another requirement was to live on the land for five years. I was given residency credit for my three years of service in the Army, so I gave notice to the government that I would give final proof on November 25, 1903. On the cold morning of November 25, 1903, my future son-in-law, W. S. Thompson, and I left the homestead, crossed the South Canadian River, and made the long ride to the courthouse in El Reno with the intention to complete the citizenship papers, go to the Land Office, and get the title for the land. I believed that only one trip to El Reno was necessary.

On arriving at El Reno, I was dismayed to learn that I couldn't get my citizenship papers that day. The court had been in session, but had adjourned until Monday, November 30th. Again, I said, "What the hell are they trying to do to me?"

Next Monday morning, we returned to the El Reno Courthouse, I swore allegiance to the United States and became a citizen on November 30, 1903. I have to admit that allegiance was not the only swearing I was doing that day. On the same day, title to the homestead was transferred to me. The land was mine. I knew my family would be able to live on this land for many years. I stood up for my rights and didn't let the government take my land."

Becoming Citizen and Landowner

Just a little more than two years after arriving in Oklahoma Territory, the Rinns completed their homestead requirements and received title to their land on November 30, 1903.[69] Lewis Rinn also became a citizen at the same time.[70] The family continued making improvements on their land, building a frame addition to the house to have six rooms and cultivating more land. The farm turned out to be productive farming land. Almost 30 years later, son Edmond Rinn, bought the farm from the estate of Marguerite Rinn and continued the ownership for another 15 to 20 years.

Lewis Rinn Land Patent
After paying $200, he was required to get his citizenship papers.

Lewis Rinn's Citizenship Certificate

Rinns Gather for Family Photo

At the time this picture was taken, Benoite Clair, Marguerite's mother, called Grandma Clair, was visiting from Baldwin, Kansas. Not speaking English, she traveled by train with a note on her coat telling her destination. The 672 square foot log house initially had four rooms, and a tarp protected part of roof.

When Marguerite's cousin, Jennie Gonon, visited from Kansas in 1903, Lewis Rinn sent samples of his corn back with her to Kansas. The local newspaper invited people to visit their office to see the corn but they appeared to think Kansas grew good corn too.[71]

Rinn Family at Homestead, Oklahoma Territory-about 1903
Front Row LR: Benoite Clair, Marguerite, Jesse, Seona, Lewis Rinn
Back Row; Lottie, Edmond, Violet, Lewis Jr., Claire, Theoda, Claude Rinn

Hazel Dell School Founded

Rinn Children attended Hazel Dell School (At first, a one room school, later a second room built as in photo)

When the Rinns arrived at their homestead in 1901, the children had no school to attend the first two years. Helen Mitchell wrote the following description of the school history:

> In 1902, a group of neighbors gathered under the shade trees to discuss the possibility of building a school for their children to attend. Since most of the residences were log cabins, dugouts, or soddies, some thought a log cabin school would suffice. Yet with vision of the future and other settlers moving west, the majority held out for a right and proper school house to be built.
>
> A group of 22 men went into Minco and signed a joint note with J. B. Pope to acquire the lumber and other supplies. Among the co-signers were B. F. Lasley, Jeff Smith, Charles Black, H. S. McDaniel, Amos Luttrell, James, Meegan, L. D. Rinn, Will DeMoss, H. E. Walje, Bob Baker, John Dix, Harve Baker, and Hugh Meegan.
>
> The original wood frame building was 25 x 40 feet facing the east. The foundation was walnut blocks cut from the Jeff Smith and H. S. McDaniel farms. Later a rock foundation was substituted. The one room school, named Hazel Dell, was completed

in time for the fall term of 1903, with 30 pupils enrolled for a six-month term. [No doubt, Edmond, Seona, and Jessie Rinn were part of the 30 students].

At first a small bell on the teacher's desk was used to summon the pupils to class. Later a belfry was built and a large bell that could be heard throughout the countryside was installed. Initially, kerosene lights were hung from the ceiling to light the school. Then carbide lights replaced the kerosene ones. The building was heated with a huge potbellied wood burning stove in the center of the room.

Enrollment continued to grow as more settlers headed west. In 1906-7 there were 61 pupils enrolled. In 1911, a second room of the same dimensions was built to the north of the original structure to care for the increased enrollment. The potbellied stoves were moved to the far north end of the first through fourth grade room and to the south east corner of the other room.[72]

Hazel Dell was located one mile north of the Rinn farm at the present-day intersection in Grady County E1140 Rd., and N2760 Roads. Three Rinn children and several grandchildren attended Hazel Dell School for the next 30 years. The school closed in 1957 and burned down in 1959.

Family Lived Near the Town of Minco

The Rinn farm, located 10 miles west and one mile north of the town of Minco, was originally in Caddo County. Realignment of county boundaries in 1911 placed the farm in Grady County.[73] Saturday afternoons found farm families, likely including the Rinns, gathering in town to visit and shop. By the time the Rinns arrived, Minco, one of the oldest towns around, had been a trading center for southwestern Oklahoma for many years. Minco was officially established on July 4, 1890, but it had settlers before that time. In 1892, the Rock Island Railroad extended its railroad from Minco to Fort Worth and soon connected north to Union City. With the opening of the lands west of Minco in 1901, the town boomed. It was incorporated in 1902.[74]

Early Minco excelled. Buyers of polo ponies came from as far away as Kansas City and St. Louis to buy ponies from the nearby ranches. The newspaper, the *Minco Minstrel*, was established in 1890 as the oldest newspaper in Oklahoma. The first corn carnival and stock show in the state of Oklahoma, attended by several thousand people, was held in Minco in 1908. Minco Academy was an early school.[75]

In the early days, Minco was a prosperous town. It had two lumberyards, three grain elevators, one flour mill, two hotels, a black smith shop, a livery barn and two banks. Various Indian camps were in the vicinity of Minco. The Kiowa and Comanches had a camp south of town, and the Caddos and Washita had a camp north of town.[76]

Minco, Oklahoma Early 1900s—looking west on Main Street

North Side Main Street Minco, Oklahoma, early 1900s.
Block where Rinn Meat Market was located
(Photos from Collection of Virgil Robbins- copy provided by Woody Woodworth)

Lewis Rinn Died in 1905

As early as 1890, Lewis Rinn applied to be put on the Disability Civil War Pension Roll of the United States government. He stated that rheumatism, caused by long marches during the war, affected his kidneys to the extent that he could not do manual labor.[77] Apparently, his health continued to deteriorate. In the winter of 1905, he suffered stomach trouble. He made out a will leaving everything to his wife, Marguerite.[78] He lay in bed for several weeks and died at 1:15 early on Saturday morning, February 11, 1905, at the Rinn farm. His obituary in the *Minco Minstrel Newspaper* said he died from catarrh or inflammation of the stomach.[79] Stomach problems may have been an inherited condition. His older brother, Phillip Rinn, died in 1881 from enteritis.[80]

His age was given as 63, however, he was actually 64 at the time of death. He was buried at the Hazel Dell Cemetery, located one mile north of his homestead and across the road from the school.[81] As a member of Knights and Ladies of Security, a fraternal and benevolent society, he had insurance benefits through that organization. He also was a member of the Select Knights, which was part of the Ancient Order of United Workmen, which was a fraternal benefit organization.[82] Lewis Rinn carried a $2000 insurance policy.[83] Present-day value would be approximately $52,000.[84]

Lewis's Life

The adventuresome and challenging life of Lewis Rinn began in Germany and ended 64 years later in Oklahoma Territory. He migrated to America as a 10-year-old with his family; served three years in the Civil War; ventured to the western frontier; worked as a butcher; married the love of his life, and fathered ten children.

Funeral Card

MINCO MINSTREL NEWSPAPER

FEB. 24, 1905, PG. 1

Louis [sic] Rinn

Louis Rinn died at his home two miles north of Leal on Saturday morning, Feb. 11, at 1:15 o'clock, after an illness of several weeks from catarrh of the stomach.

Mr. Rinn was born in Germany and came to this country when but a boy. He served three years in the Civil War as a private and was honorably discharged July 13th, 1864.

He was employed as a butcher for the government at Camp Supply, where he was married, afterwards moving to Kansas where he lived until the opening of the Caddo country. He drew a lucky number and secured a choice claim on which he has since resided.

He was a member of Select Knights and Knights and Ladies Security carrying insurance in both orders. He was 63-years-old and leaves a wife and nine children. The family are widely known and respected, and many friends join the Minstrel in extending sympathy to the bereft.

THE EVENING HERALD NEWSPAPER

February 13, 1905, page 2

Ottawa Kansas

Ben D. Lillard received a telegram Saturday announcing the death of Lewis Rinn, which occurred at Leal, Oklahoma.

Mr. Rinn formerly lived in Franklin County. At one time he owned a quarter section of land which afterward became Silkville.

Mrs. Rinn was a daughter of M. Clair who was associated with M. de Boissiere in the silk industry. He lived here until three years ago when he moved to Leal.

Mr. Rinn was nearly sixty-three years old. He carried two thousand dollars insurance in the Select Knights and Ladies.

Chapter 5

Marguerite Holding Family Together

On a cold winter day in Oklahoma Territory, Marguerite Rinn's family gathered by her side as they wept for the loss of their father and husband, Lewis Rinn. Marguerite knew that no matter what the future held, her family would be by her side, and their support would give her the strength to carry on. At the age of 48, Marguerite had a lot of responsibility placed on her shoulders. She had been married almost 29 years to a man who adored and pampered her. She mourned the death of Lewis Rinn and missed him. But there was little time to grieve because her nine children, ranging in age from 27-year-old Lottie to 9-year-old Jessie, needed her. Lewis, Edmond, Seona, and Jessie were still minors. None of the older children were married. Someone needed to manage the 160-acre farm and Marguerite lost no time arranging her affairs.

She sent a telegram to Ottawa, Kansas, to the Select Knights and Ladies insurance company informing them of the death of Lewis Rinn and requested her $2000 life insurance benefit, equivalent to approximately $52,000 in 2020 dollars.[85] On November 28, 1905, Marguerite applied for and received a widow's pension from the government for her husband's military service.[86] Prior to his death, Lewis made out a will leaving everything to Marguerite.[87] With help, she continued to farm the 160-acre homestead turning it into a productive farm. A less rustic two-storied house replaced the original homestead house.

Older Daughters Married

Soon after the death of Lewis, the older Rinn children began to marry and leave home. Lottie, Claire, Violet, and Theoda were all married early in 1906. Lottie married Frank Pond on January 5, 1906.[88] Clair married Ralph Fultz on January 10, 1906.[89] Violet married William Thompson on January 9, 1906.[90] Theoda married William Martin on June 27, 1906.[91]

Rinn sisters married in 1906, L-R: Theoda, Violet, Claire, Lottie

Surrounded by Family

Most of Marguerite's family lived nearby, and on Sundays, family gathered to enjoy Marguerite's delicious meals. Lottie and Claire had lived in El Reno, but after her marriage, Lottie and husband moved back to the Hazel Dell community. Violet lived in the nearby Leal community. At various times, Marguerite's sons-in-law helped with the farming, especially Will Martin. The Martins lived in a separate house on the property for many years. Bruce and Jessie Arthur as well as Lewis, Jr. later lived there.

Marguerite with Loving Family-about 1906
Seated LR: Edmond, Marguerite, Lewis Jr., Claude
Standing LR: Ralph and Claire Fultz, Seona, Frank and Lottie Pond, Jessie,
Will and Theoda Martin William and Violet Thompson missing from photo.

The Party-line

Because they had a telephone, the family never felt isolated even though they lived 11 miles from the town of Minco. They could step to the oak phone hanging in the corner of the living room, pick up the ear piece, turn the crank on the side of the phone until the operator in Minco answered. Then they could tell her who they wanted to talk to.

In the early days of phone service, most homes were on a party line where several residences shared the same phone line. This practice continued until the 1960s especially in rural areas. Party lines in rural areas, such as Hazel Dell, became part of the community culture. Even though numerous families shared the same line, they all had their own distinctive ring such as two short and one long that everybody could hear. When the party line was in use by someone, others on the line could pick up the phone and listen in. Eavesdropping was a source of entertainment and gossip. In the close-knit community of Hazel Dell, everyone knew their neighbors, but they knew them best from listening in on the party line.

Some people, knowing others were listening, tried to fool their neighbors by exaggerating a story to give them something to talk about. Eavesdroppers often gave themselves away when they revealed information that they could only have known from listening to the phone conversation.

The Rinn sisters loved to frustrate their neighbors when they got on the party phone line and chattered in French. You could hear the receivers clink down when they were on the line speaking in French. These spirited, mischievous, sisters learned to speak French from their French grandmother and loved to annoy their neighbors and often giggled as they heard the disappointed listeners hanging up.

Son Brought Sweetheart to Meet Marguerite

As remembered by Grandson Scott Rinn

After the death of his father, oldest son, Claude, left home and established a meat market in Enid, Oklahoma. In 1908, at the age of 27, he met 22-year-old Anna Mabel Reeves, a young woman selling millinery products for a company headquartered in Kansas City. He courted young Anna whenever her travels brought her to Enid. He finally convinced her to make a trip with him down to Minco to visit his mother, Marguerite. Claude coached Anna with a smattering of French in order that his young sweetheart could impress Marguerite when they were first introduced. Prepared with a French phrase carefully rehearsed with Claude, Anna, upon being introduced to Marguerite, and surrounded by most of Claude's sisters, said in perfect French: "Va te faire foutre" or "Kiss my ass." It was a memorable introduction to the Rinn family for Anna, and quite a hit among Claude's sisters. Anna must have forgiven Claude, for a wedding followed on December 31, 1908, with the mother of the groom in attendance.[92]

French Customs

The family carried on many French customs. Great-granddaughter, Paula Phillips, wrote:

The family continued the French custom of kissing as a greeting. One in-law was overheard to comment, when entering the room at a reunion, "For heaven's sake, everybody stay put. I don't want to have to kiss any of you twice." Marguerite Rinn was often embarrassed at the Hazel Dell community picnics when her brood gathered around her food and didn't want to eat any other. She was considered as one of the best cooks around. Known as a spirited and lively bunch, the Rinn clan stuck together and didn't seem to need or want others.

The Rinn farm was the scene of many happy gatherings. Often on a summer Sunday afternoon, horses with fancy buggies could be seen tied to the hitching bar, waiting patiently while their owners, married Rinn sons and daughters, neighbors, and friends, played croquet in the Rinns' front yard. When the weather forced them inside, the young people crowded together to play cards. When Grandma Clair, adored by the younger family members, visited from Kansas, she would join in the card playing. Although she never became fluent in English, one thing she could say loud and clearly was. "You cheat! You cheat!" The industrious Marguerite would keep the hungry group filled with her famous goodies. On holidays, all the family seemed to come home.

Everyone thought Margaret Rinn was so cute with her strong French accent. She was short, but was a nice-looking woman and always so well dressed. She liked to laugh and have fun.[93]

Hazel Dell Church

On February 9, 1909, neighbors established the Hazel Dell Missionary Baptist Church of Christ. Services were held at the school house which was one mile north of the Rinn farm. Families arrived in their buggies for Sunday school and then stayed for church before returning home for the noon Sunday dinner. Many church and school social activities took place there. Marguerite's family, the Clairs, were Catholic. But when she came to Oklahoma, she eventually joined the Hazel Dell church, where her children attended.

Seven Grandchildren in Three Years

Donald Pond was born October 22, 1906. Pauline Fultz was born December 10, 1906. W.S. Thompson was born October 14, 1907. Frank Pond was born July 24, 1908. Marguerite Martin was born July 2, 1909. Raymond Rinn was born February 2, 1910. Gene Pond was born March 31, 1910.

Marguerite's Grandchildren about 1911,
LR: W.S. Thompson, Marguerite Martin, Donald Pond, Frank Pond, Gene Pond,
Pauline Fultz

Grandma Clair Visited

Benoitc Clair, Marguerite's mother, lived in Baldwin, Kansas, with her youngest daughter, Theodie (Clair) Jardon. She liked to come down to Oklahoma on the train to visit with the Rinn family, sometimes for long visits. Because she never learned to speak English, she had a note attached to her coat with directions saying where she was going. Since she refused to learn English, her grandchildren learned to speak French. On the 1910 census, she is listed as residing with Marguerite on the farm.⁹⁴

Family Scattered

By 1910, Oklahoma was a state and Marguerite, aged 52, lived in Washington Township in Caddo County. Later, the county boundary changed putting her homeplace in Grady County. She identified herself on the census as a farmer who owned her own mortgaged farm. Her mother, 77-year-old Benoite Clair, was in the household, visiting from Kansas. Children, Edmond 18, Seona 16 and Jessie 14 all attended school, and lived with her. Daughter Theoda and husband William Martin, and granddaughter Marguerite were neighbors along with the McDaniel, Pederson, and Kushmann families.⁹⁵ Son, Lewis Jr., was living nearby in Lone Rock Township, Caddo County, working as a farm laborer for the William Gordon family.⁹⁶

Her older children lived farther away. Lottie (Rinn) Pond and family lived in Eugene, Oregon, then Florida before returning to Oklahoma. Claire (Rinn) Fultz and family lived in Cresell, Kansas. Violet (Rinn) Thompson and family lived in Ninnekah, Oklahoma. Claude Rinn and family lived in Enid, Oklahoma.[97] Seona Rinn married Ruel Daggs on November 3, 1913 and moved to Iowa.[98]

Four Generations-about 1911,
FR:Benoite Clair, Marguerite (Clair) Rinn,, BR: Pauline Fultz, Claire (Rinn) Fultz

Bonne Temps

Marguerite Rinn got a new piano in 1912.[99] Numerous social events took place at the Rinn home, making use of the piano as friends and family often visited. Parties for young people at the Rinn place were described in the local newspaper.

> **Mrs. L. Rinn Entertains**
>
> A large crowd of young folks enjoyed an Easter party at Mrs. Rinn's. A picnic dinner had been prepared and they flocked to the timber where tables were set for the occasion. They didn't leave eaven a bone for the poor dog. An egg hunt was a feature of the event, the prize being won by Hazel Miller. A large swing added enjoyment and the young folks engaged in playing games, (some spooning too we suppose) or whatever fancy dictated. The day seemed made especially for this occasion, after the unsettled weather of late, and they enjoyed it to the utmost.

1911 Easter Party

> **Hallowe'en Party**
>
> The Ghosts kept Hallowe'en at Miss Jessie Rinn's Saturday evening. About 7:30 the white robed figures (with the proverbial black cat) met in the parlor, which was lit by jack-o-lanterns. After some music the ghosts repaired to the lawn where quiet games were indulged in. This was followed by a ghost march and unmasking. A delicious lunch was served, the cakes and cookies being representations of pumpkins. The dining room was tastefully decorated in orange and black, the jack-o-lanterns shedding a soft radiance and

1914 Halloween Party

Troubles

Marguerite's two youngest sons, Edmond and Lewis Jr. got in trouble. The local newspaper reported on February 16, 1912, their arrest along with two other young men for stealing a neighbor's cattle. They pleaded guilty. Family lore says Lewis took most of the blame. Edmond was placed on probation, and Lewis was sentenced to reformatory school.[100]

Mother Died

The last few years of her life, Benoite Clair was paralyzed and bedfast and unable to travel to Oklahoma. Marguerite made trips to Kansas to visit her dear mother when she could get away. An Ottawa, Kansas, newspaper reported on July 23, 1913, Marguerite Rinn visiting Mrs. L.C. Stine and Mrs. Herron of Ottawa before going to Baldwin to visit her sister and mother.[101] On January 3, 1917, Benoite Clair passed away and was buried in the Catholic Cemetery in Baldwin, Kansas.[102]

Marguerite's Endless Work

Year-round Marguerite worked—cleaning, cooking, sewing, doing laundry, and caring for family, all without indoor plumbing, electricity or refrigeration. Extra chores in the summer added to her workload. In a letter to her daughter, Seona Rinn Daggs, Marguerite Rinn wrote: "*Since I came back home my garden was so needy that I spent most of my time hoeing the weeds a little each day. Then I would play out. My rheumatism bothers me quite a little in my knee.*"[103]

She planted vegetables such as tomatoes, beans, peas, turnips, potatoes, onions, okra, corn and carrots. There were also fruit trees. Weeding the garden was a constant challenge. If there was not enough rain, all her work would be wasted. Harvesting the garden was backbreaking work.

With the help of her daughters, Marguerite canned and preserved vegetables and fruit during the hot, humid July and August weather. Despite the steamy kitchen, they had fun giggling and chatting in French as they put the produce into sterilized jars, placed a rubber ring on and screwed down the lid before placing them in large pans of boiling water on the wood burning stove. The water bath would cook and preserve the food. Completed jars were then taken to the cellar to be stored for wintertime use.

She fed the harvesting crews. In June, crews of men traveled from farm to farm with a big machine that threshed wheat and oats. Neighbors in the Hazel Dell community also gathered to help with threshing. Marguerite's daughters and neighbor women helped her cook meals for the hungry field workers of at least 10 or more men who usually spent several days threshing at the Rinn farm. Marguerite Rinn's family remembered her as an excellent cook. Neighbor women helped each other, but it was a contest for most of the women in the community to try to put on the best meals for the harvesting crew each summer. No doubt, the harvesters liked her food.

Marguerite, an excellent seamstress, taught her daughters to sew and make their own clothes and quilts. She made a crazy quilt which is still in the possession of the family. It is not known when it was made, but crazy quilts first became popular in the 1880s and were a fad for many years. Irregular shaped pieces of velvet, satin, tulle or silk fabric were joined by fancy embroidery stiches in seemingly no pattern to form a "crazy quilt". The quilts were extremely labor-intensive. A Harper's Bazaar article from 1884 estimated that a full-size crazy quilt could take 1500 hours to complete. [104]

*Crazy Quilt Made by Marguerite Rinn
(in possession of Gene Rinn family, photo by Janelle Richardson)*

Sons Went to War

Lewis and Edmond Rinn both registered for the World War I draft in June, 1817. Lewis married Leoda Sanders on May 31, 1918.[105] One day later he enlisted in the army on June 1, 1918. Serving in the United States, he was discharged February 11, 1919.[106] Edmond enlisted and served in the 358th Infantry, 90th Division departing New York on June 20, 1918 to serve in combat in France.[107] Marguerite and her family received postcards from the Red Cross saying he arrived safely. His unit was in some of the heaviest fighting of the war participating in the Meuse-Argonne successful campaign in the fall of 1918. The division remained on the front lines attacking for more than 69 days sustaining a total of 7,549 casualties until the Armistice of November 11, 1918, earning the name of "Tough Ombres".[108]

Edmond wrote home on January 27, 1919, saying he didn't know when he would be coming home, but he hoped it would be soon. He wanted to see his mother and find out how everyone was getting along.[109] Late in May 1919, he got his wish as he sailed from France and arrived back home in Oklahoma in June 1919.

I Went to France to Fight—Summer of 1918

Edmond Rinn was proud of his service during WWI
He loved to tell the story of how he got out of being a translator

Told in The Imagined Words of Edmond Rinn

Edmond Rinn WWI
Served in Army 1918-1919

"I went to France to fight, not talk. Proud to defend my country, I was 26-years-old when I became a private in the United States Army during the Great War (First World War). I remember it was hard leaving home in Oklahoma as my mother, Marguerite Rinn, fussed over me and cried. I am her youngest son. Even my usually vibrant, giggly sisters were sobbing, kissing me goodbye. They acted like I wouldn't return. I was tall, lean, strong, and well trained and I knew I would be okay in battle. Didn't my own father, Lewis Rinn, survive three years in the Union Army during the Civil War?

We were encamped near a small French village. My commander called me in and said, "Private Rinn, I understand you speak French." Yes," was my reply because my Mother and Grandmother were from France and my family spoke French at home especially when Grandma Clair visited. The commander said, "I need you to leave your company so you can become our translator."

I thought this sounds like a boring, uneventful job. Damn, I wanted to be in the trenches with my buddies. But an order was an order so I saluted and replied, "Yes sir."

Then I was told, "Your first assignment is to go into the village and introduce yourself to the local bar keeper. Say that your commander has ordered drinks for the troops. Tell him to serve the enlisted men one drink each and to serve the officers all the drinks they want.

I wondered how I was going to get out of being a translator. Suddenly I had an idea. Off to the village I went. I found the bartender and greeted him. In my best French, I told him that my commander had ordered drinks for his men. The enlisted men could have all the drinks they wanted, but the officers were restricted to one drink.

It didn't take long before my commander called me in. He said, "Rinn, it doesn't appear that you are suited to be a translator. I am afraid that you will have to rejoin your regular combat company."

"Yes sir," I replied as I turned and left the room, hoping that he did not see the pleased look on my face. I was going to fight after all."[110]

LOTTIE (RINN) POND DIED IN 1920

By 1920, Edmond Rinn was home from the war and he and Jessie lived at home with Marguerite. Theoda and Will Martin and family lived nearby in a house on the Rinn farm. In October 1920, Marguerite received word that her oldest daughter, 42-year-old Lottie Pond, was very ill. Immediately, she and several of her daughters made the trip to Neodasha, Kansas, where the Ponds were living. It was too late, Lottie died of peritonitis from complications of a miscarriage on October 25th.[111] She left four boys ages four to fourteen. Concerned about the boys, Marguerite decided to bring 4-year-old Tom Pond, and 10-year-old Gene Pond back to Oklahoma to live with her and Jessie. At the age of 63, she took on the added responsibility of caring for two young boys. Jessie and all the aunts helped out. It was long remembered in the Hazel Dell community how engaging little Tom Pond was at the school programs when his grandmother dressed him up.

Marguerite Lived Alone

Edmond Rinn married Susie Dobbins on April 9, 1921.[112] Jessie Rinn married Bruce Arthur on November 26, 1922.[113] By 1924, Gene and Tom Pond rejoined their father and brothers in California. Marguerite lived alone in her farmhouse although her daughters were nearby.

Marguerite in Front of House-1920s, (house in background believed to be an abandoned earlier house)

Marguerite Kept in Contact

Marguerite stayed in contact with her sister, Theodie (Clair) Jardon and niece, Jeanne Gonon, in Kansas. She wrote to her grandson, Gene Pond in California and daughter, Seona, in Iowa. An old letter was found in a box of pictures and cards kept by Seona Daggs reads as follows:[114]

> *Minco, Okla*
>
> *July 4, 1924*
>
> *Dear Seona & family*
>
> *I have no excuse for not writing sooner. I just neglected it since I came back home. My garden was so needy that I put most of my time weeding the weeds a little each day. Then I would play out. My rheumatism bothers me quite a little in my knee then other trouble. I eat well. Got good appetite and that's all. I get so nervous at times but I think will be all ok when you and Ruel get here and Vera Mae.*
>
> *This is the fourth but we all stayed at home. Jessie has Aileen D. Moss visiting her so today they had Claire Cole and family and Violet and family for dinner. I guess they had a good time. We had plenty of rain lately and crop is looking fine. I want you when you come to make your headquarters with me. And if you can drive my car we will ride some. All I need is a driver. I have also a Edison so we will have music. I will do all I can to make it pleasant for you all. Tell Ruel not to back out but come as soon as he can. We saw Ray Daggs last Sunday. He passed us by in a car all by himself. I was surely surprised.*
>
> *Well dear one won't write any more but will talk you to death when you get here. Marguerite broke her wrist cranking a car a week ago Sunday. Has to wear her arm in a sling for three weeks. She is getting along fine. The rest are all well.*
>
> *Frank Pond is still in California. Eugene writes often. Both Donald and Francis are working in a Barber Shop and Eugene is Boot Blacker. So you see they are all busy. Tell Ruel to come and shoot squirrels. We have plenty of them and tell Vera Mae to come down and she will play croquet with Louise and Marguerite.*
>
> *Now come. I am anxious to see all of you. With lots of love to you all. A big kiss to Ruel and big hug to you and Vera Mae. Write when you are going to start.*
>
> *Lots of Love,*
>
> *Maman*

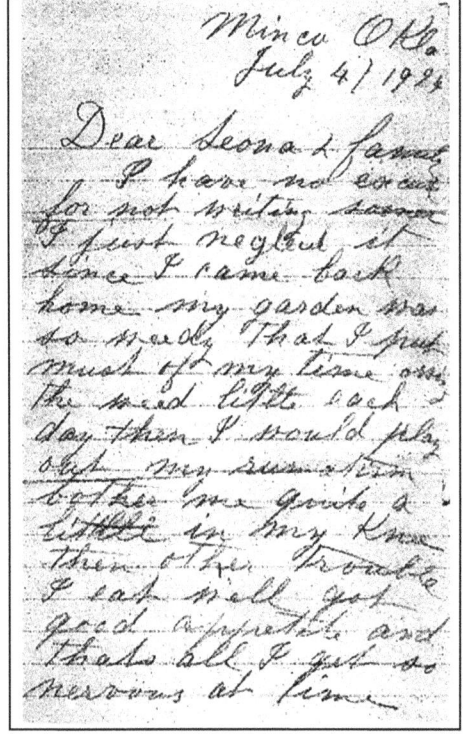
Handwritten Page

Marguerite's letter is well-written considering English was not her native language. [To facilitate reading, a few corrections have been made such as periods placed at end of sentences and capitals at beginning.] In the letter she is trying to convince the Daggs family to come visit, but it is not known if they came down to Oklahoma that summer. She mentions she has a car, but since she says she needs a driver, likely she did not drive. She also owns an Edison record player.[115]

Marguerite (Clair) Rinn Died in 1929

Marguerite's health began to deteriorate with diabetes. After 1927, it became necessary for Marguerite to be taken care of by her daughters. She stayed in the homes of Claire (Rinn) Cole and Jessie (Rinn) Arthur before being moved down to Minco to Violet (Rinn) Thompson's home so Dr. Jesse Little could look after her. After about a year and a half of poor health, Marguerite died on May 14, 1929, at the home of her daughter, Violet Thompson, in Minco, Oklahoma.[116] She was almost 72 years old and had many friends in the community.[117] Her services were held at the First Baptist Church of Minco, where the church was full to overflowing. A member of the Hazel Dell Baptist Church, her pastor, Rev. Barker, along with Rev. F. D. Grover of the Methodist Church and Dr. E. H. Sawyer, conducted the services. The funeral procession left Minco and traveled to the cemetery, where more friends and neighbors joined the family. She was buried beside her beloved husband, Lewis Rinn, at the Hazel Dell Cemetery one mile north of the Rinn farm.[118]

Her Life

Marguerite (Clair) Rinn's life began in a French city and ended 72 years later in rural Oklahoma. She migrated to America as a 12-year-old with her family, lived in a commune in Kansas, ventured to the western frontier, married an older German who was the love of her life, and mothered ten children.

Postscript

Less than a week after Marguerite's death, youngest son, Edmond Rinn, petitioned the Grady County Court on May 20, 1929, to be appointed administrator of the estate of Marguerite Rinn. Heirs were her eight surviving children plus the four grandsons of her deceased daughter, Lottie (Rinn) Pond. By November 27, 1927, the estate, worth approximately $7500 was settled.[119]

Edmond Rinn purchased the 160-acre Rinn farm, worth $6500, from the heirs. He retained ownership for approximately the next 20 years. Not a farmer, Edmond leased out the land. Originally, Jessie (Rinn) Arthur and husband Bruce lived there until about the early 1930s and later Lewis Rinn Jr. and family lived there.

Rinn farm as photographed in 1996

In Memory of Mrs. Margaret Rinn

Minco Minstrel, May 24, 1929

The concourse of friends who assembled at the Baptist Church Wednesday, May 16th, evidenced the respect and love that was entertained for our old friend, Mrs. Margaret Rinn, long a resident of (Caddo) and Grady County.

The church was full to overflowing, many persons waiting on the outside to express their sympathy to the bereaved family. The flower pieces were many and beautiful, mute tokens of the love in which she was held.

Mrs. Margaret Rinn was born in France, July 29th, 1858, coming to this country with her parents when about twelve years old. At the age of nineteen she was married to Lewis Rinn. To this union ten children were born, one dying in infancy.

When this country was opened for settlement, with her family she made a home on the farm in Hazel Dell, which through the years was the scene of many happy gatherings. She still resided on the home place when overtaken with her fatal illness. Her devoted husband departed this life in 1905. She was essentially a mother and held her family together, until, one by one, they were able to go into homes of their own.

Mrs. Rinn joined the Hazel Dell Baptist Church several years ago, and by her daily walk and conversation, her friends knew she was led and supported by the only Hand that uplifts and holds the widow and her orphan children.

Mrs. Rinn bore with great patience the long months of illness that were spent at the homes of her daughters, Mrs. Cole and Mrs. Arthur, passing away at the home of her daughter, Mrs. Thompson. Everything was done for her that good nursing and the best medical attention could furnish, but the end came May 14th.

Mr. Barker, her pastor, Rev. F.D. Grover of the Methodist Church, and Dr. E. H. Sawyer conducted the services. Mrs. Frank DuBois, in her sympathetic manner, sang the beautiful hymn, "There'll Be No Night There," and other old favorites of Mrs. Rinn's were sung by a mixed choir from the town churches.

After friends and relatives had looked upon her dear face for the last time, the remains were laid to rest beside the husband in Hazel Dell Cemetery, where many friends and neighbors, who could not attend the Minco service, awaited the coming of the funeral cortege, and said the last "Rest in Peace" as the casket was lowered into its final resting place.

All of the children, except Mrs. Frank Pond, were at their Mother's funeral; Mrs. Pond (Lottie Rinn) preceded her mother in death eight years ago, leaving her husband and four little boys when she was called to her home on high.

The children who are left to mourn their cherished mother are Daniel C. Rinn of Enid, Lewis Rinn of Billings, Edmund Rinn of Chickasha; Mrs. E.V. Cole, Mrs. W.S. Thompson and Mrs. Rual Daggs, of Minco; Mrs. William Martin and Mrs. Bruce Arthur of Hazel Dell, and twenty grand-children. All of the wives and husbands of Mrs. Rinn's children were present at her funeral, except Mr. Frank Pond, whose home is in California. He visited Mrs. Rinn while she was ill at the home of Mrs. Cole.

Among the grand-children present were Miss Pauline Fultz of Muskogee, Marguerette and Louise Martin of Hazel Dell, Miss Vera Mae Daggs of Minco, W.S. Thompson, Jr., of Norman, and Tom Pond. Her sister, Mrs. Jardon of Baldwin, Kansas, visited with Mrs. Rinn at the home of Mrs. Cole this winter but was unable to come on account of a serious accident in her own home.

Marguerite's Death Certificate Signed by Dr. Little, Diabetes Cause of Death at Age of Almost 72

Rinn Grave Marker

*Grandchildren & Great Grandchildren Visit Rinn Grave 2009
LR: Janette (Pond) Lusk, David Daggs, Jim Daggs, Jim Peavler, Bill Thompson, JoAnn (Pinkston) Gedosh, Janelle (Pond) Richardson*

Hazel Dell Cemetery where Lewis and Marguerite Rinn are buried.

Rinn farm

PART II

Marguerite's Early Life

"Mama was born in France and came to Kansas as a girl to live in a commune."

~Jessie Rinn, youngest daughter

Chapter 6

MARGUERITE CLAIR BORN IN FRANCE

A life filled with adventure and challenges began on July 29, 1857, in Saint Etienne, France, for Marguerite Clair. Marguerite's parents, 26-year-old Jean Claude Clair, and 24-year-old Benoite (Gonon) Clair lived at 14 rue de l'Heurton near the Place du Peuple, a square near the center of the city, where she was born at home. Her father and fellow ribbon weavers, Pierre Policard, and Pierre Forest, went to Hotel de Ville (City Hall) to register the birth of his first-born child the following morning.[120]

Marguerite Clair's Birth Certificate-1857

> In the year one thousand eight hundred fifty-seven the 30 July, at nine hours and a half in the morning did, in front of us, deputy and officer of civil status of the city of St. Etienne (Loire), appeared Claude Clair, age of twenty-six years, velvet-maker, street of Heurton 14, who to us introduced a child of sex female born in his home yesterday at nine hours in the evening, of him declaring and of Benoite Gonon, his wife, age of twenty-four years, housewife, of which he gave the first name of Marguerite, all made and read in the presence of Pierre Forest, age twenty-one years, velvet-maker, street of Gris 20, and Pierre Policard, age twenty-eight years, street of Chappes 36. Undersigned with us and the father.
>
> Bangy (probably the deputy)
>
> Clair, Forest, Policard

English translation of Marguerite's Birth Record

Marguerite Lived in Thriving French City

Marguerite Clair's family lived in the thriving industrial city of Saint Etienne located in eastern central France about 35 miles southwest of Lyon.

Saint Etienne Industries

Coal mining, arms manufacturing, and silk ribbon production took place in Saint Etienne since the 16th and 17th centuries. One of the most important industrial centers of France, it could be considered the French birthplace of the Industrial Revolution, having the first French railway by 1827, and the first sewing machine by 1830. At the time of Marguerite's birth, Saint Etienne prospered as a center for textiles and metal crafts. It was a well-established city with shopping, churches, and many cultural activities with a population of about 94,000.[121]

Saint Etienne was famous in the 19th century for its fabric and ribbon production. Weavers replicated artistic patterns through the use of a binary punch card system or early computer system to set up the looms.[122] Marguerite's father, Claude Clair, worked as a velvet and silk ribbon weaver.[123] These craftsmen were considered among the elite and most skilled workers and best paid workers in the city. Ribbon production was a cottage industry that took place in workshops in large homes. The weaving was not automated. Taffeta, serge, satin or velvet ribbons in several hundred different colors were produced. With as many as 15,000 looms in Saint Etienne and surrounding area, they dominated French and international markets during the mid to late 1800s. Workshop houses, called fabriques, were located near the town center and contained large high windows to let in light.[124] Possibly, Marguerite's parents met in one of the workshops as Claude worked as a velvet weaver and Benoite worked as a ribbon folder at the time of their marriage in 1856.[125]

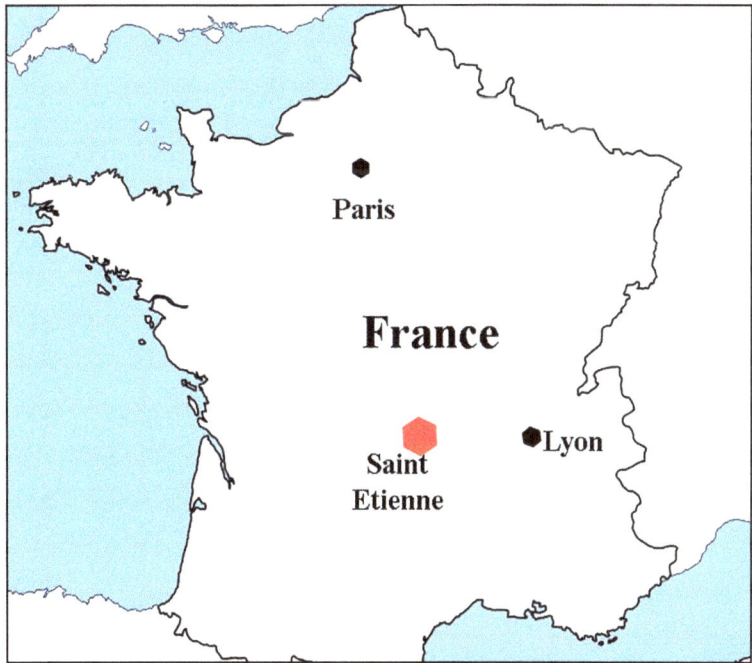

Clairs Lived in Saint Etienne

Arms manufacturing played an important role in Saint Etienne. Countless firearms for military and civilian use were produced. Marguerite's maternal grandfather, Pierre Gonon, was a blacksmith with a successful business.

One of the largest coal mines in France, the Couriot Mine, was located in Saint Etienne. The first railroad in France was built in 1827 to transport coal from the local mine to Paris.[126]

Saint Etienne Churches

Built in 1445, the oldest Catholic church called Grand 'Eglise, is located in the historical center of the city. The local sandstone used for construction has taken on and eroded appearance over time. A painting within the church depicts individuals pleading with the Virgin Mary to protect the populace from the plague of 1629 in which almost half the population perished.[127] The second oldest church in Saint Etienne, Notre-Dame (1669), is located in the arms and manufacturing district and near the Clair home. It likely was the parish the family attended.[128]

Weaving Workshop called Fabrique (photo Discover Saint Etienne)

Modern Rue de l'Heurton, street where Clairs lived.

*Grand 'Eglise Church Built about 1445,
(Postcard photo)*

*Statue Honoring Ribbon Makers
Saint Etienne City Hall*

Place du Peuple near Clair Home

*Marguerite Clair's Descendants
Visited Saint Etienne City Hall in 2000*

Marguerite Clair's Family

Immediate Family: Marguerite's parents, Claude Clair and Benoite Gonon, married on August 2, 1856 in Saint Etienne.[129] A month before Marguerite turned three, her brother Pierre, joined the family in June 1860. By that time, the family had moved out of the center of the city farther south to the LeMont, Valbenoite parish neighborhood.[130] Shortly after the Clairs left France and settled in Kansas, their last daughter, Theodie, was born on January 19, 1870.[131]

Parents

Father's Family: Marguerite's father, Jean-Claude Clair, known as Claude with the last name of Clair, Clerc or Le Clair, was born on January 3, 1831, in the village of Saint-Jean-Bonnefonds about three miles east of Saint Etienne.[132] His family soon relocated to Saint Etienne where his father worked as a tailor. His father, Jean-Fleury Clair, passed away in 1836 when Claude was 5-years-old.[133] His mother, Marguerite Jacques Clair, later married Francois Gourd, a carpenter.[134]

Claude Clair,
(picture taken in Saint-Etienne)

Benoite Gonon,
(unknown picture location)

Mother's Family: Marguerite's mother, Benoite Gonon, was born in the village of Le Chambon on January 5, 1833. Her father, Pierre Gonon (1803-1871), was a blacksmith in the industrial village just southwest of Saint Etienne. Her mother was Catherine (Chapelon) Gonon (1805-1890).[135] Later the Gonon family moved into Saint Etienne where they had a successful blacksmith business. Benoite was the second oldest daughter in the family. Family tradition said that her oldest sister, possibly named Louise, became a nun and was a mother superior in her order.[136] Her other sister, Virginia, married Pierre Forest, a silk ribbon maker and likely the Pierre Forest signing Marguerite's birth registration.[137] Brother Antoine Gonon and family migrated to America and joined Claude and Benoite in Kansas.[138]

Grandparents

Catherine Chapelon 1805-1890   *Pierre Gonon 1803-1871, Successful Blacksmith*

The German Bachelor & the French Girl

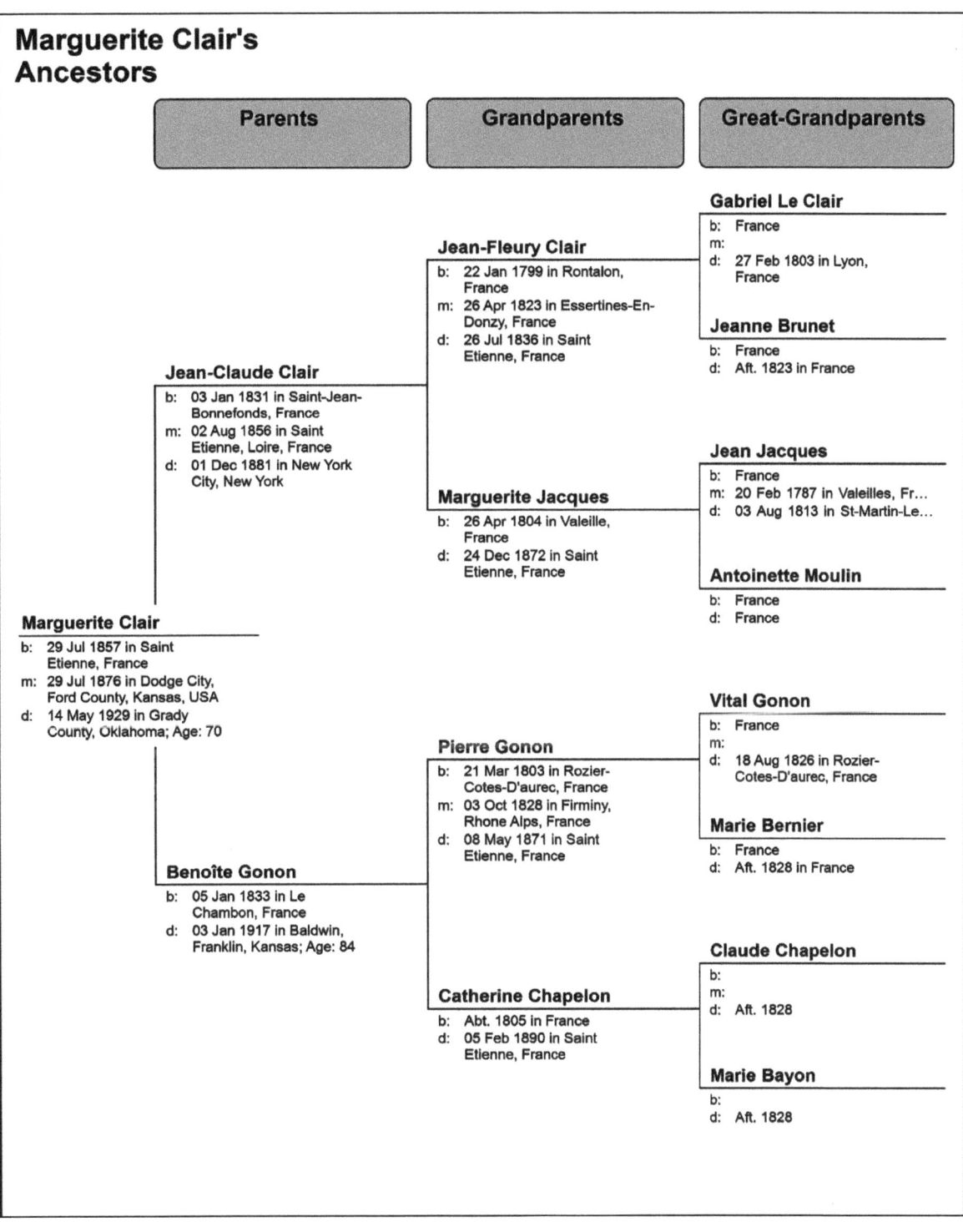

Marguerite Clair's Ancestors

Parents

Jean-Claude Clair
- b: 03 Jan 1831 in Saint-Jean-Bonnefonds, France
- m: 02 Aug 1856 in Saint Etienne, Loire, France
- d: 01 Dec 1881 in New York City, New York

Marguerite Clair
- b: 29 Jul 1857 in Saint Etienne, France
- m: 29 Jul 1876 in Dodge City, Ford County, Kansas, USA
- d: 14 May 1929 in Grady County, Oklahoma; Age: 70

Benoîte Gonon
- b: 05 Jan 1833 in Le Chambon, France
- d: 03 Jan 1917 in Baldwin, Franklin, Kansas; Age: 84

Grandparents

Jean-Fleury Clair
- b: 22 Jan 1799 in Rontalon, France
- m: 26 Apr 1823 in Essertines-En-Donzy, France
- d: 26 Jul 1836 in Saint Etienne, France

Marguerite Jacques
- b: 26 Apr 1804 in Valeille, France
- d: 24 Dec 1872 in Saint Etienne, France

Pierre Gonon
- b: 21 Mar 1803 in Rozier-Cotes-D'aurec, France
- m: 03 Oct 1828 in Firminy, Rhone Alps, France
- d: 08 May 1871 in Saint Etienne, France

Catherine Chapelon
- b: Abt. 1805 in France
- d: 05 Feb 1890 in Saint Etienne, France

Great-Grandparents

Gabriel Le Clair
- b: France
- m:
- d: 27 Feb 1803 in Lyon, France

Jeanne Brunet
- b: France
- d: Aft. 1823 in France

Jean Jacques
- b: France
- m: 20 Feb 1787 in Valeilles, Fr...
- d: 03 Aug 1813 in St-Martin-Le...

Antoinette Moulin
- b: France
- d: France

Vital Gonon
- b: France
- m:
- d: 18 Aug 1826 in Rozier-Cotes-D'aurec, France

Marie Bernier
- b: France
- d: Aft. 1828 in France

Claude Chapelon
- b:
- m:
- d: Aft. 1828

Marie Bayon
- b:
- d: Aft. 1828

Chapter 7

Clairs Coming to America

Marguerite Clair was 12 when her life changed. Her parents decided to leave France and come to America to help establish Silkville, a commune in Kansas located south of Ottawa and near the recently founded town of Williamsburg. In the early years, life was hard with poor lodging, living conditions, and other privations during the establishment of the commune.

Leaving France

The Clairs applied for emigration in 1868 in Aarau, Aargau Canton, Switzerland, which was about 300 miles from their home in Saint Etienne. It is not known what the family was doing in Switzerland. Were they living and working in Aarau or passing through?[139]

The details of their travels are not known, but the Clairs likely traveled to the port of Le Havre and crossed the Atlantic in a steam-sailing ship. They then took a train to Ottawa, Kansas, arriving after many weeks of travel. No American passenger arrival records have been found for the family. They may have traveled to Canada and crossed into the United States. But no Canadian immigration or border crossing records are available for 1869.[140]

The First Years a Rugged Adventure

How did Marguerite feel about leaving her friends, family, and the lively city of her birth to go to a strange country and live in a small farming community?

The Story of Marguerite Clair Arriving in Kansas

TOLD IN THE IMAGINED WORDS OF MARGUERITE CLAIR

Hissing and still spraying out coal-laden smoke, our train lurches to a stop next to a makeshift railroad station. My nine-year-old brother, Pierre, and I jump up and down shouting, we are here at last. We gather our belongings and step onto the wooden siding. My father leads the way. It seems a lifetime ago since we left home in Saint Etienne, France, braved the ocean crossing and traveled here to Ottawa, Kansas. I am more weary, sticky, and grimy with each stage of the journey.

I look about. Across the tracks, I see wood frame storefronts and houses scattered along the dusty road. Several horses and wagons are tied to hitching posts beside the wooden sidewalks. This must be Ottawa, said to be the largest town around, so different than back home.

We load a wagon with our few trunks—everything we brought from home. I look around as we ride down the bumpy track for more than an hour to the south. I see nothing—no buildings, no fences, no planted fields. Then I notice movement and a slight humming sound. It's the endless grass moving with the wind.

Finally, we stop at a small primitive house in the middle of the prairie. Maman says this is going to be our home for a while until we get our own place. What is living in the wilds of Kansas going to be like?

Ernest de Boissiere comes out to greet us and in the French manner, kisses all of us on both cheeks. He is the person who encouraged Papa to come to America to help him establish a commune, called Silkville, with everyone working together and sharing the profits. I'm told this grandfatherly looking gentleman, with his full grey beard, is actually a very wealthy French philanthropist who dreams of establishing a self-supporting community. He already purchased more than 3500 acres where silk production and silk ribbon making will be the focus of the community. Mama and Papa, skilled ribbon weavers, will set up and work the looms.

Later, I hear Papa and de Boissiere talking about their grand plans for the community. Monsieur de Boissiere laughs and says, "Of course these first few years will be too rugged for even the devout socialist to come here." Well, I certainly understand that. Twilight spreads across the vast sky on the lonesome prairie. I feel like this is going to be an adventure. I can hardly wait.

Clairs Settle in Franklin County, Kansas

By June 1870 the Clairs lived at Silkville in the same household with 59-year-old Ernest de Boissiere and six other individuals from France, Ireland and Canada. Marguerite's younger sister, Theodie Clair, had been born within months after their arrival in America. Marguerite likely helped take care of the baby. Other French families lived nearby.[141] A year later, Marguerite had cousin playmates. Ten-year-old Catherine and younger sister Jeanne Gonon arrived from France. Their parents, Antoinie and Marie Gonon, were Marguerite's aunt and uncle related on her mother's side.[142] Initially, the Gonons lived at Silkville where Antoinie worked as a blacksmith and weaver. Later they moved to nearby Osage County.[143]

Ernest De Boissiere Founder of Silkville

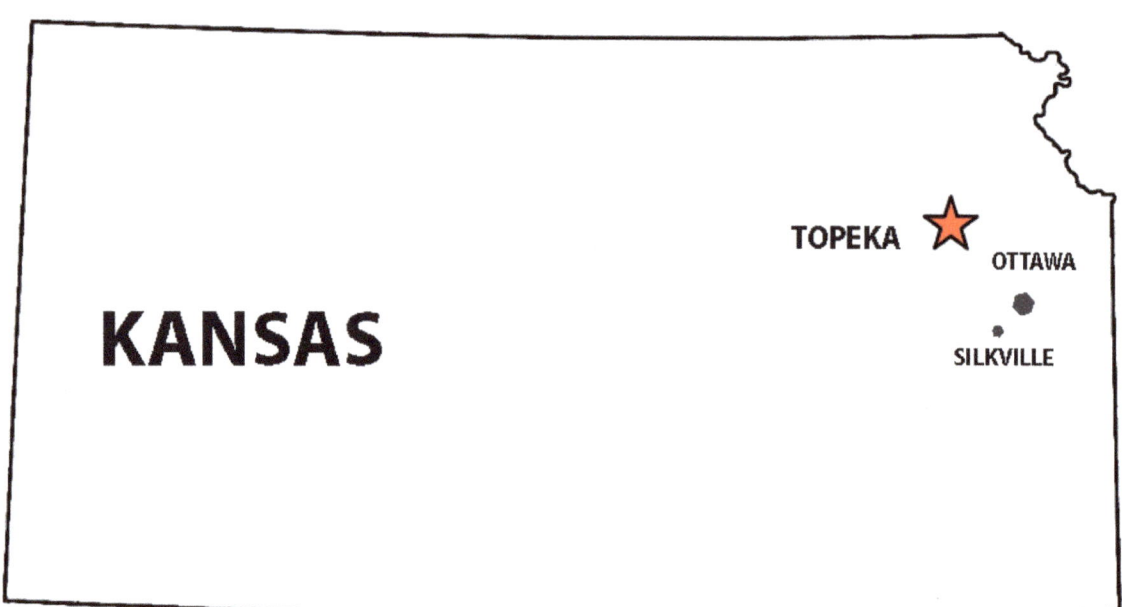

Silkville Located Southwest of Ottawa, Kansas

Maternal Uncle, Antoinie Gonon   *Marie Gonon*

Photos of the Gonon Family were taken in Saint Etienne, France prior to 1871.

Claude Clair Establishes Weaving at Silkville

Despite the rugged conditions, Claude Clair proceeded with setting up the looms and beginning the production of silk ribbon. To establish the silk producing community, 8000 mulberry trees were planted and silk worms imported. Clair's work in weaving silk ribbons became successful, producing 260-300 yards of ribbon per day. At the Centennial Exposition in Philadelphia in 1876, displays of silk production from Silkville received first honors.[144]

Structures Built at Silkville

On the commune, a large three-story house with 60 rooms was built for about 100 workers to rent rooms where they lived and ate in the common dining room. Referred to as the "Chateau," it was at that time the largest manor in the state. It contained a library filled with 2500 books in four different languages.[145] Additional stone structures included barns, an icehouse, a winery, and a cocoonery.[146]

Silkville Ribbons Kept in Rinn Family Artificacts

Mulberry Trees Remaining at Silkville (2008)

Eventually, about 40 French workers joined the commune from time to time. At first, there was no school, but soon a county school was established at Silkville where Marguerite Clair could attend school and learn English.[147]

Silkville Schoolhouse Built 1881 (photo by Janelle Richardson 2003)

Clairs Built Home

Workers were allowed to live separately at Silkville. Early in 1872, Claude Clair signed a 20-year land lease with de Boissiere for $10 a year and built a stone house for his family to live in, and farm buildings to raise livestock and crops to support themselves. Eventually, he leased about 25 acres and made improvements worth about $2300.[148] De Boissiere bought the buildings back in 1883.[149]

In 2007, the remains of the Clair house still stood in a field at the corner of present-day Arkansas and Cloud Roads, about a quarter mile diagonally across the field from the chateau. Trees surrounded the small stone farmhouse and no outbuildings remained. With a collapsed roof and insecure walls, the more than 125-year-old structure appeared ready for demolition.

Remains of Clair House at Silkville (2007)

Life at Silkville Commune

The first few years, very few outsiders visited Silkville, but local people were curious about what went on there. Lem Woods, who wrote an article based on the Fogle family memories for a Ottawa newspaper in the 1930s, described a party held at the commune. He wrote, *"Early in the summer of 1874, notices were printed in the Ottawa and Burlington papers that on a certain Sunday, excursion trains would run to Silkville, and everybody was invited to come and see how silk was made. A large crowd came to visit, eat, and dance. They all had a good time and were impressed."* Writers wrote about the spacious buildings and the good production of the cheese factory. The orchards were thriving and the vineyards were producing wine.[150]

Sometime in 1874, Marguerite's father went back to France, possibly to acquire weaving supplies. He returned to New York City aboard the ship France on November 17, 1874.[151]

Clairs Travel to Ottawa and Leavenworth to Shop

The small village of Williamsburg, established in 1864 was within 3 miles of Silkville. The larger town of Ottawa, the county seat of Franklin County, was located about 25 miles northeast. From Silkville, the Clairs could flag down the train in order to go into the town of about 2900 people to shop.[152] The frontier-style town did not resemble their well-established thriving French city of Saint Etienne. On occasion, the Clairs journeyed 80 miles to the larger city of Leavenworth which had a population of about 17,000 people.[153]

Marguerite Clair-about 1875

Sometime around 1875, Marguerite Clair had her photo taken by S. Bauer, photographer and portrait painter, on 409 Shawnee Street, Leavenworth, Kansas.[154] The photo shows slender 18-year-old Marguerite with her long dark hair pulled back from her face. Her fancy dress is embellished with silk ribbons, likely woven by her father, at the neck and bodice. Her solemn expression may reflect her determined, strong personality, but she is also remembered as a fun-loving, energetic person.

Downtown Ottawa, Kansas- 1870s, (Kansas Historical Society)

Marguerite Goes To Indian Territory

Claude Clair realized his oldest daughter, 18-year-old Marguerite or Maggie as the family called her, should improve her English. She needed to be away from those French-speaking people at Silkville. He had a friend, Philipp Huret, who owned a rooming house down in Indian Territory at Camp Supply, who needed a cook for the summer of 1876. Her mother had taught her to be a good cook and seamstress. It was here that the vivacious, dark-haired, brown-eyed Marguerite Clair went to work. Her life changed forever. She met Lewis Rinn, fell in love and was married on July 29, 1876.[155] It is not known what Claude Clair's reaction was to the marriage. It may be an understatement to say he was somewhat surprised when he sent his daughter to learn English, and she married a German a few months later.

Chapter 8

Living at Silkville Commune

In 1869 Claude Clair, a silk ribbon maker from Saint Etienne, France, came to Silkville to set up and operate the looms.

Silkville, was not a town, but was an attempt to form a socialistic commune on a large tract of land of 3500 acres, located about 20 miles south of Ottawa, and three miles south of the small town of Williamsburg, Kansas, in southwest Franklin County. Today it is a working ranch called the Silkville Ranch.

Silkville Established as Commune

Referred to as Kansas Prairie Home or Kansas Cooperative, the farm was first established in 1869 when a wealthy Frenchman, E.V. de Boissiere, purchased the unimproved land to form a commune based on the Fourierist socialistic principles.[156] It may not have been his original intention to specialize in silk manufacture. In an interview in 1870, de Boissiere said he came across a party of French silk weavers in Chicago last year who were out of work, and he offered them a chance to start their trade on his premises.[157] Likely, one of the silk weavers referred to was Claude Clair, However, Clair family tradition neither confirms or refutes that they first met de Boissiere in Chicago. Eventually the farm became known as Silkville. De Boissiere had a vision that Silkville would be a self-sustaining rural cooperative educational and industrial community where participants would share the wealth.

Current Silkville Ranch Sign
Janelle Richardson (2009)

De Boissiere, an intelligent, portly man in his 60s, loved books, music, and helping the underprivileged. Born June 9, 1810 near Bordeaux, France, into an aristocratic family, he made a fortune of his own through fisheries and forestry. For political reasons, he left France in 1852 and came to the United States. After a failed attempt to help establish a school and orphanage for black children in New Orleans, he looked elsewhere to implement some of his humanitarian ideals. He found his location in Kansas. He bought the land and poured money into the establishment of Silkville.[158] During the early years when accommodations were crude, he endured hardships.

The commune was intended to be self-sustaining. A prospectus, issued in 1873, invited socialists and others to join. Workers were considered associates and were remunerated in proportion to their productivity. Destitute persons were not admitted. Each worker was required to give a $100 deposit and to provide for their own needs and to pay rent for their rooms two months in advance. The style of living was to be frugal and inexpensive.[159]

De Boissiere, Founder of Silkville

Silk Ribbons Produced

The production of silk and silk ribbons became one of the main industries. Seventy acres of the choicest land were set out with mulberry trees to feed the silk worms. A large stone building 25x80 was built in October 1870 to house the looms and the location where the worms were to be kept.[160] By the year 1872 the three looms at Silkville had a capacity of making 224 yards of ribbon a day. Interest in silk production spread throughout Kansas.[161]

De Boissiere exhibited his manufactured silk products at the 1876 Centennial Exhibition in Philadelphia where his products were awarded first prize over entries from all over the world. De Boissiere took a personal interest in exhibiting his silk products. He was known to have taken charge of displays at fairs in Bismarck Grove, near Lawrence, and the state fair in Topeka.[162]

Silkville Prospectus, Circulated 1873

Mulberry Trees

Silkville Diversified

Mr. Charles Sears, who was the former president of the Fourierist North American Phalanx, came from New Jersey and became the commune manager in 1875. His son, Charles T. Sears, developed the farm, orchards, and stock raising. The farm was well stocked with the finest bred cattle and horses. To generate income, a cheese factory was established. Large vineyards and orchards were put out as they they engaged in farming of all kinds. Workers from all over the world (France and Sweden primarily) came to be part of the community. Most workers did not stay long preferring to invest in private property rather than a communal enterprise. It is believed that no more than about 40 or 50 workers lived at Silkville at one time—maybe even fewer.[163]

1876 Centennial Exhibition Award for Ribbons (Display Franklin County Old Depot Museum)

Many Buildings Built

Substantial improvements, which were very modern for the time, took place at Silkville. A limestone fence four feet high was built around the entire place, making a total of 15 miles of fence. All the buildings were limestone. They built a large cheese and creamery, a building for a blacksmith shop and workroom, several large barns and sheds for stock. A total of 600 acres were put in cultivation, and 500 acres of prairie-grass were reserved as hay land. The remainder was used as pasture land that was supplied with water from a dozen artificial ponds.[164]

Silkville Limestone Barn
photo by Janelle Richardson (2003)

Silkville Manor, the "Chateau" for Workers

For workers, a three-story, 60-room stone manor house, 36 by 95 feet, was completed in 1874 where people shared meals in the dining room but lived in separate apartments with their families. It was so grand that the local people referred to it as the "château" but de Boissiere preferred the less pretentious name of "phalanstery"—the home of a "phalanx". It was said that as many as 100 people could be housed there with its spacious parlors and large dining room. A library of 2,500 books, the largest in Kansas at that time, was established. Silkville was also a flag stop on the Kansas City, Burlington and Santa Fe Railroad.[165]

In the early days, school was conducted above the creamery building. A stone school building was built and dedicated in October 1881at the north corner of the property for the children at Silkville.[166]

Some Workers Leased Land

Some workers were allowed to lease land and build their own homes paying about $10 to $36 a year for a land lease. Claude Clair leased 20 acres and built a house for his family. His property was diagonally southwest across the field from the main manor house, located at the junction of two section roads now known as Arkansas and Cloud Roads.[167]

Silkville Workers, Ranch manager Charles Sears on right, Sears children in front

Remainder of Silkville Stone Fence

Commune Failed

Silkville failed as a commune in part because not enough associates could be attracted to live the communitarian way of life and the cooperative labor scheme. Many associates left the farm because they could make higher wages elsewhere. So, people had to be hired and paid wages. The competition for silk products from the Orient was growing, making the Kansas silk industry unprofitable. Silk could be imported cheaper than workers could make it at Silkville. Claude Clair, the main weaver, died in 1881. From 1881 on, the silk activities at Silkville were curtailed and only retained on an experimental basis until it was abandoned in 1886.[168]

The philanthropist's dream came to an end. De Boissiere went home to France. General agriculture and stock raising did continue for a period of time but it was clear that the idea of a cooperative commune was dead.

De Boissiere Deeded Property to Odd Fellows

In 1892 at the age of 82, de Boissiere returned to Kansas. He knew his idea for a commune had failed, but he wanted to devote his Kansas land for the greatest possible good for humanity. When he made his wishes known, many representatives from charitable institutions visited him hoping to secure the property. Representatives of the Independent Order of Odd Fellows of the state of Kansas approached de Boissiere about devoting his property to establishing an orphans' home and industrial school for the children of deceased Odd Fellows of the state of Kansas. First de Boissiere studied the constitution, laws, and literature of the order. He stated that he did not want to give the property to the Odd Fellows so they could sell it. He wanted it kept together. Terms were agreed upon and the property was deeded to the Odd Fellow's Grand Lodge of Kansas.[169]

On May 11, 1892 Ernest Valeton de Boissiere, Frenchman who founded Silkville, deeded all his real and personal property, amounting to nearly $150,000, to a trust for founding an I.O.O.F. orphans' home. The gift included a 3,100-acre farm with nine stone buildings, an apple orchard, a mulberry grove and a walnut grove.[170]

On Oct. 11, 1892 the Grand Lodge accepted the gift and voted to enact a $1.50 per capita tax to its members to support the running of the home. Some members opposed establishing the home and legally fought the case. In 1894, the Grand Lodge passed resolutions severing its connection with and withdrawing further support from the home. De Boissiere died on January 12, 1894.[171] Certain lawyers felt that the rejection by the Grand Lodge nullified the original transaction and the title of the property should revert to the heirs of de Boissiere. A long legal battle developed over the ownership of Silkville. L.C. Stine of Ottawa, who was a great friend of de Boissiere, and who had gotten him to deed the place to the Odd Fellows, made a grand and noble fight for the order.[172]

Legal Battle Over Ownership

Once the I.O.O.F. had repudiated the gift, ownership fell into the courts. The law firm of Troutman and Stone of Topeka claimed that de Boissiere's sister, Madame Corrine Martinelli, was the heir to the property. In 1896 James Troutman, for $4500, got Madame Martinelli to sign a quitclaim deed to their law firm. Litigation commenced and was in the courts for years. The Odd Fellows claimed that de Boissiere intended the property to be orphans' home and had deeded the property to them, that they had invested $34,000, and that the lawyers fraudulently got Madame Martinelli to deed over the property. The Supreme Court of Kansas on January 9, 1903, decided in favor of Troutman and Stone declaring the original trust deed to the Odd Fellows void. On September 1, 1910, Troutman and Stone, Topeka lawyers, sold Silkville, near Williamsburg, for $130,000 to a private party. The property remains, in 2020, undivided but not held by a charitable organization as de Boissiere wished. It is one of the biggest blocks of land in eastern Kansas.[173]

Post script: On April 29, 1916, the Silkville original manor house, valued at $40,000, was partially destroyed by fire. It was rebuilt at about one-third of the original size and used as a farm house. During the 1950s, the John Netherland family purchased the Silkville Ranch. In 2003 the ranch, still containing the original land, was sold to Jim and Joe Bichelmeyer.[174]

Descendants Gathered at Silkville in 2007

June 2007, descendants of Marguerite (Clair) Rinn, her sister Theodie (Clair) Jardon, and her Gonon cousins gathered at Ottawa, Kansas, for a family reunion. More than 40 family members visited Silkville and Williamsburg to view where their family lived in the late nineteenth century.

Rebuilt Manor House (photo by Janelle Richardson 2003)

Rinn/Clair/Gonon Family Descendants Visit Silkville 2007

PART III

Lewis's Early Life

"Papa was born in Germany and came to Pennsylvania as a young boy. Later he served as a soldier in the Civil War.

~Jessie Rinn, youngest daughter

Chapter 9

Ludwig "Lewis" Rinn Born in Germany

Born on April 21, 1841, in a small crowded cottage in Heuchelheim, Germany, Ludwig Rinn was baptized days later at the Martinsgemeinde Church in Heuchelheim.[175] Natives of Heuchelheim, his parents, farmer Ludwig Rinn and Anna Maria (Kröck) Rinn, were both 33 years old.[176] Franz Albrecht Vitriarius, the pastor of the church, his father, Ludwig Rinn, and Jacob Steinmueller, Georg Loeber, and Katharina Elisabetha Henkelman signed his baptism record.[177] He was the fifth child and second Ludwig born to Ludwig and Anna Maria (Kröck) Rinn. The first Ludwig, born in 1836, lived just nine months before he died in July 1837.[178]

Ancient baptismal urn outside Heuchelheim church

Martinskirch, Heuchelheim, Germany

The Birth Register of the Evangelical Congregation

of

Heuchelheim, District of Giessen, Grand Duchy of Hesse, Germany

In the year of Christ, 1841, April 21, in the morning at 11 o'clock, by credible notification of **Ludwig Rinn**, *citizen and farmer here, was born to his wife* **Anna Maria,** *born* **Kröck**, *their fifth child, a son, the 4th son, who was baptized the 25th of the same month and who received the name* **Ludwig**.

Witnesses of the baptismal were:

1. ***Jacob Steinmueller***, *citizen and farmer, here.*
2. ***George***, *of the late* ***Johannes Loeber***, *citizen and farmer, here, unmarried son, here.*
3. ***Katherina Elisabetha***, *of* ***Ludwig Henkelman***, *citizen and farmer, here, unmarried daughter.*

Above signed the present protocol, written by the preacher, who conducted the baptism.

Franz Albrecht Vitriarius, *Preacher*

Heuchelheim Martinskirch Center of Village Life

The Heuchelheim Martinskirch (Church), site of Ludwig Rinn's baptismal, is in the center of the village with the church spire seen from some distance. Parts of the building date from 1279 when the church was Catholic. After the reformation in 1526, the church became Lutheran but retained the name Martin from Saint Martin. In the past, life centered around the church. Babies, brought to the church by their fathers a few days after birth, were baptized. Marriages were announced, approved, and conducted in the church by the pastor. Children, trained in the church tradition, were confirmed.[179]

During the Thirty Years War (approximately 1618-1648) much of the village burned, many people died, and the church records prior to 1648 destroyed. Originally a war between Protestants and Catholics, the war developed into a struggle between European powers especially in central Germany. One of the most destructive conflicts in history, millions died from violence, famine and plague.[180]

The Rinn and Kröck families had three sons who survived the war. About 3500 people currently live in Heuchelheim. Sixty-five families have the Rinn last name making them the largest family and the Kröck family the second largest.[181]

The Evangelisch Martinskirche. (Lutheran Church) holds birth, marriage and death records from 1649 to present.[182] They include Ludwig Rinn's earliest recorded ancestors, Johann Heinrich Rinn (1648-1699), and[183] Lorenz Kröck born 1670.[184]

Rinn Family Lived In Heuchelheim

There was no country called Germany in 1841. The area now known as Germany was a loose confederation of 39 sovereign states.[185] The village of Heuchelheim was part of the Grand Duchy of Hesse. In 1871, the area was unified and became Germany. Today it is a municipality in the district of Giessen, in Hesse, Germany. It is located about 40 miles north of Frankfurt near the city of Giessen and north of the Lahn River. From Frankfurt to Heuchelheim, the land is flat, but everything to the north of the Lahn River is rolling hills with lots of forest and some castles. Thirty miles northeast of Heuchelheim is where the brothers Grimm produced their fairy tales. Picture Little Red Riding Hood in a forest and that might describe the area.[186]

Originally, Heuchelheim had many half-timbered houses built next to the road with an inside, private courtyard. There was a fire in 1881, but the buildings were rebuilt to resemble the original houses. In 1660 there were 47 families with 212 people living in Heuchelheim. Each family had many children which increased the population. By 1805 there were 904 people living in 164 houses. The population increased to 1344 in 1851. The population increase made it more difficult for families to make a living off the same land that once supported fewer people.[187]

Village Children Attended School

Most of the villagers could sign their names on the church records during the 1800s. Both girls and boys attended school, but the men had more legible writing which might indicate more education. By the time a child was 14, school was

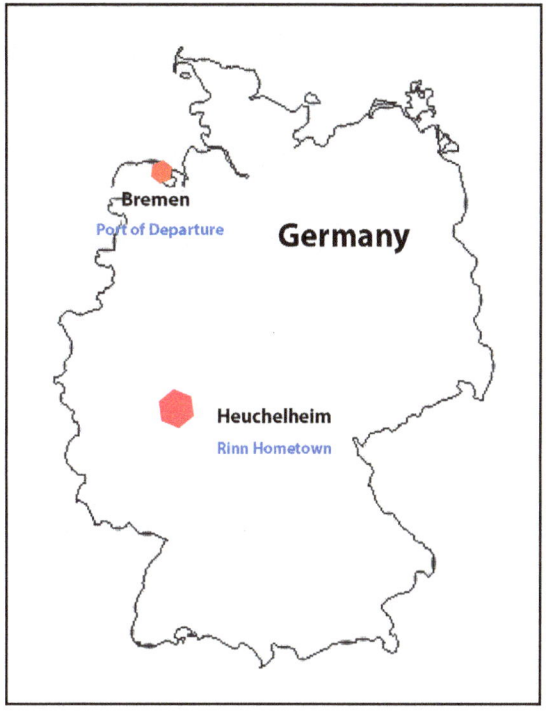
Heuchelheim located in present-day Germany

completed. The school had many children. In 1831, there were 195 children and one teacher. In 1851, a second teacher was added for the 250 children.[188] No doubt, Ludwig "Lewis" Rinn was one of the students.

Traditionally most of the men in the village farmed, but the town a few tradesmen such as butchers, black smiths or weavers. Families lived in the village and farmed land outside the town center.

By 1849, the Rinns had four growing boys and one daughter. Times were hard. The family barely eked out a living as farmers on their plot of land just outside the village. It would be impossible to make a living in the future if the land was split into four plots for each of the boys. There was much talk of opportunity in America. Oldest son, 21-year-old Jacob, left home and went to America. His friend and distant cousin, Jacob Kröck, went with him.[189] In the summer of 1851, Jacob sent word that he was established in Allegheny City near Pittsburgh, and the rest of the family should come to Pennsylvania. The town records list Ludwig Rinn as granted permission to emigrate in 1851 taking 5,000 florins with him.[190]

Heuchelheim Schoolhouse

Half-timbered Heuchelheim house

Leaving Home

The Story of Ludwig "Lewis" Rinn Leaving Germany

Told in the Imagined Words of Ludwig "Lewis" Rinn

I do not want to leave my friends, but time is running out. Papa says we must leave Germany and go to Amerika. We always do what Papa says.

My name is Ludwig and I am 10 years old. I live in our little house in the small town of Heuchelheim, which is near the Lahn River in central Germany. My best friends and I love to play in the fields when we are not working or going to school. All of us have learned our numbers and letters sitting next to one another in the two-storied schoolhouse where Herr Schneider and his assistants are stern schoolmasters. What will my friends do when I am gone?

I know almost everyone in Heuchelheim. I am told that Papa's family, the Rinns, and Mama's family, the Kröcks, have lived here for hundreds of years and I am probably related to most of the 1500 people in town. People speak to me as I go down the narrow, cobbled streets that are lined with old half-timbered houses that have high pitched gabled roofs.

Papa farms a small plot of land outside the village, but times are hard and we never have enough for our family of seven. A couple years ago Papa thought conditions might improve. But there was a failed revolution and now there is no hope for us boys.[191] *Everyone is talking about the "good life" in Amerika. My older brother, 21-year-old Jakob, left home two years ago and went to Amerika.*[192] *We have heard from him and he says he is learning to be a butcher and he has a place for us near Pittsburgh.*

I don't think Mama wants to leave Heuchelheim. She looks frail and far older than 43. One day I saw her crying as she was telling the other women about our plans.

It is August 1851 and Papa busied himself all summer selling our furniture and his farm tools and land. He seems pleased because the 5,000 florins he has will pay our traveling expenses and get us started in the new land.[193]

It is time to go before winter comes. My older brother Philip, who is 16, and my sister, 18-year-old Catherine, will miss their friends, but they seem excited to go to Amerika. My younger brother, eight-year-old Heinrich, and I wish our friends could go with us. We are scared and excited at the same time. Papa says the trip is going to be long and hard. We must go to the port at Bremen to get passage on a sailing vessel to Baltimore and then take a train to Pittsburgh. What will it be like to see the ocean, travel on a merchant vessel and go to a new land and live in a city?

Finally, we are ready to leave. I say goodbye to my friends. Heinrich and I crawl onto the back of the oxcart where our few possessions are stored. We begin our long journey north. We look back on our village. For a long time, I can see the tall steeple of the Martinskirch as it slowly disappears, gone forever.

Martinskirch Not Gone Forever

Ludwig Rinn never returned home. But almost 150 years later on May 15, 2000, three generations of his descendants returned to Heuchelheim and visited the church, viewed the old church record books, and met distant Rinn and Kröck relatives.

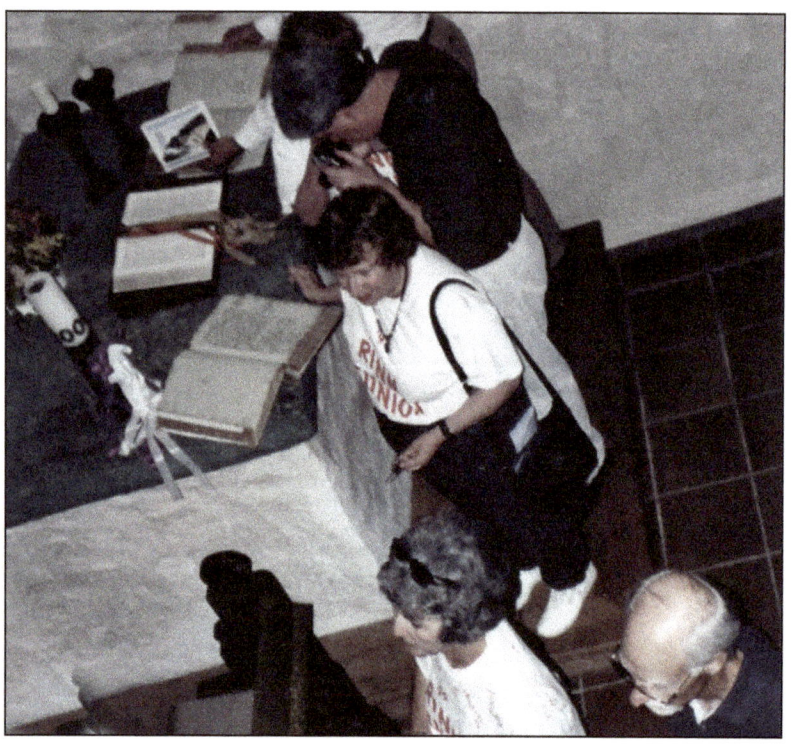

Family viewing Heuchelheim Church records

Rinn descendants at Heuchelheim Church 2000

German Ancestors of Ludwig "Lewis" Rinn

Parents / Grandparents / Great-Grandparents

Ludwig "Lewis" Rinn
- b: 21 Apr 1841 in Heuchelheim, Hesse, Germany
- m: 29 Jul 1876 in Dodge City, Ford County, Kansas, USA
- d: 11 Feb 1905 in Grady County, Oklahoma; Age: 64

Parents

Ludwig Rinn
- b: 03 Mar 1808 in Heuchelheim, Hesse, Germany
- m: 16 Apr 1829 in Heuchelheim, Hesse, Germany
- d: Unknown in USA

Anna Maria Kröck
- b: 16 Apr 1808 in Heuchelheim, Hesse, Germany
- d: 19 Feb 1852 in Allegheny City, Allegheny County, Pennsylvania, USA

Grandparents

Johannes Rinn
- b: 02 Mar 1780 in Heuchelheim, Hesse, Germany
- m: 27 Mar 1806 in Heuchelheim, Hesse, Germany
- d: 10 Jul 1811 in Heuchelheim, Hesse, Germany

Elisabeth Margrete Schneider
- b: 04 Jan 1781 in Heuchelheim, Hesse, Germany
- d: 25 Dec 1857 in Heuchelheim, Hesse, Germany

Jacob Kröck
- b: 08 Feb 1787 in Heuchelheim, Hesse, Germany
- m: 28 May 1807 in Heuchelheim, Hesse, Germany
- d: 23 Nov 1858 in Heuchelheim, Hesse, Germany

Katharina Elizabetha Henkelmann
- b: 17 Mar 1787 in Heuchelheim, Hesse, Germany
- d: 19 Jan 1820 in Heuchelheim, Hesse, Germany

Great-Grandparents

Johannes Rinn
- b: 01 Nov 1755 in Heuchelheim,...
- m: 06 May 1779 in Heuchelheim,...
- d: 11 Mar 1808 in Heuchelheim,...

Christine Weil
- b: 04 Mar 1750/51 in Heuchelheim, Germany
- d: 24 Apr 1808 in Heuchelheim, Germany

Johann Ludwig Schneider
- b: Abt 1765 in Germany
- m: Abt 1785
- d: Germany

Anna Elizabeth Sack
- b: Abt 1765 in Germany
- d: Germany

Jakob Kröck
- b: 16 Jul 1751 in Heuchelheim,...
- m: Heuchelheim, Germany
- d: 30 Mar 1821 in Heuchelheim,...

Anna Elisabeth Reuschling
- b: 13 Feb 1756 in Heuchelheim,...
- d: 23 Feb 1804 in Heuchelheim,...

Heinrich Henkelmann
- b: 04 Nov 1760 in Heuchelheim,...
- m: Heuchelheim, Germany
- d: 19 Sep 1836 in Heuchelheim,...

Kathrine Elisabeth Romer
- b: 26 Jul 1762 in Heuchelheim, Germany
- d: 19 Mar 1828 in Heuchelheim, Germany

Chapter 10

RINNS COMING TO AMERICA

Saying goodbye to family and friends, Ludwig Rinn's family left Heuchelheim in late summer 1851 beginning their journey to America. The municipality granted emigration permits and created a list of emigrants leaving for America between 1849-1904. Brother Jacob Rinn, age 20, and Jacob Kröck, age 20, left in 1849 and took 150 florin each. Lewis Rinn's father, Ludwig Rinn IV, left in 1851 taking 5,000 florin which was the largest amount of assets of any of the emigrants.[194]

```
Rinn, Ludwig IV. - Landwirt
Mit ihm wanderten aus seine Ehefrau
und vier Kinder.
Ausreise: 1851 - Vermögen: 5.000 fl.
```

English Translation:
Rinn, Ludwig IV-farmer
With him emigrated his wife and four children.
Departure: 1851, assets: 5000 fl.

Father, 44-year-old Ludwig Rinn, emigrated with his and wife, Anna Maria, and 18-year-old daughter Catherine Elizabeth, and sons Philipp 12, Ludwig "Lewis" 10 and Heinrich 8.[195]

Traveled to Bremen

They traveled 100 miles north to Bremen and then to the port of Bremenhaven. This new port, completed in 1848, had trade agreements with the ports of Baltimore and New Orleans to transport American tobacco and cotton cargoes to Germany. The trading vessels needed to fill their ships for the return trip to America so they offered low fares to emigrants.[196] Between 1851 and 1885 more than 220 people left Heuchelheim for America.[197]

No details of the Rinn's journey to America are available, but their trip may have resembled Emil Gilbert's family who sailed from Bremen to Baltimore in 1848. Herr Gilbert described the trip in a letter to friends in Germany:

> *We reached Bremen and found a place to stay. Days later we left Bremen on a riverboat and sailed to Bremberhaven, where the American three-masted schooner Madison was to take us aboard. This part of our trip was the worst.....*
>
> *We set sail on May 11. In the North Sea, we encountered a storm and many were seasick.... A woman and a small child died underway and were buried at sea. On July 12, we at last reached Baltimore. We wanted to land immediately but had to wait for inspection by a doctor to determine whether we had brought any infectious diseases with us. ....*
>
> *On the 15th, we took the train from Baltimore via Strassburg and York, to Columbia, Pennsylvania.... From Columbia we took a canal boat to Pittsburgh, via Harrisburg, Lewistown, and Holidaysburg, then via Freeport. We arrived in Pittsburgh on July 23.*[198]

Traveled on Sailing Vessel, *Ocean*

The Rinns set sail on the Danish merchant sailing ship, *Ocean*, with captain Johann Elias Janseen and 244 other German emigrants. The square-rigged vessel, built in 1850, had three masts and measured 131 feet long and 32 feet wide.[199] Designed to carry cargo from Baltimore to Germany, it carried German emigrants on the return voyage in the fall of 1851. The exact German departure date of the *Ocean* is not known, but sailing vessels usually took from four to eight weeks to cross the Atlantic. The Rinns arrived at the port of Baltimore on October 21, 1851.[200]

Ocean Manifest Listing of Rinn Family

Rinns traveled on sailing vessel Ocean.
Courtesy Mystic Seaport Museum

Rinns Settled in Allegheny City, Pennsylvania

Allegheny City, located on the northside of Pittsburgh, was called Deutschtown in the 1850s because of the large immigrant German population. By the time the Rinn family arrived in 1851, the city no longer was a town surrounded by agriculture but a growing city with manufacturing, breweries, tanneries, slaughterhouses, a soap factory, sawmills and cotton mills. Tenement houses nestled between shops and factories. Residents could not avoid seeing, hearing, and smelling all the industrial activity. Prior to the Civil War, cotton mills were the city's largest industry where workers began a 5 a.m. and worked into evening. By 1860, the population increased to 28,702. The growth of the iron and steel industry took place after the Civil War.[201]

Anna Maria (Kröck) Rinn Died

Not long after the Rinns made their way to Allegheny City, Ludwig's mother died on February 19, 1852. The death is recorded in the St. Paul's German United Evangelical Church burial records.[202] This church, an essential part of the North Side German community, was located on Canal Street.[203]

Number	Name	Birth Location	Birthdate	Death date	Burial date
200	Rinn	Heuchelheim	17 April	19 Feb	20 Feb.
	Anna	Grand Duchy Hesse	1808		
	Maria				
	Born, Kröck??				

1852 death of Anna Maria Rinn recorded in St. Paul's Church records.

Not quite eleven, Ludwig found himself in a strange country with no mother. Ludwig, called Lewis in America, likely attended school for a short time where he learned English. During this period, children completed their schooling and began working during their teen years. Daughter, Jessie Rinn, told the following story about what happened to her father, Lewis, when he was about 12 years old: *"Papa ran away from home because his father beat him with a chain. When his stepmother came looking for him, she begged him to come back home."*[204]

Never Again—The Story Of The Beating

Told in the Imagined Words of Lewis Rinn

I am hurt, cold, and hungry, but I am not going home. I defied Papa, and in a fit of anger, he gave me a thorough beating with a chain. I was afraid he was going to kill me. It will not happen again.

My stepmother just came looking for me. She begged me to come home. She said, "If you come home, I will make your Papa promise he will not beat you again.

It is hard to know what Papa might do. Times have been hard for him since we left Germany and came to America. I remember Tuesday, October 21, 1851, when we finally sailed into the port of Baltimore. A doctor came on board to check to be sure we did not have any diseases, and then all of us 244 German immigrants landed.

Our family, Mama and Papa, my sister, my two brothers and myself, were weak and weary but glad to finally arrive in America. We made our way to Pittsburgh and then across the river to Allegheny City, where my oldest brother, Jacob, had a place for us.

I love America and am beginning to speak English and learn the ways of this new land. Here, I am called Lewis instead of Ludwig. Papa, a farmer from our small village, has not done so well. First, Mama, age 44, took sick and died just four months after we arrived. Getting used to the large, noisy, crowded city and finding work is hard for him him. Papa remarried and now his wife is pregnant.

Papa is often angry at me. I am now in my teens and have my own plans and ideas. Papa still acts like he is in the old country. He has to know that he cannot beat me. Never again.

No American Records Found for Father, Ludwig Rinn

No census, naturalization, marriage or death records, have been found for the father, Ludwig Rinn, in Pennsylvania nor elsewhere in the United States. Since the mother, Anna Maria Rinn, died in Allegheny City in 1852, and other family members lived there, likely all the family settled in Allegheny City, but the immigrant father created no records during his lifetime.

Brothers, Jacob and Henry Rinn, appear on the 1860 census records living in Reserve Township, Allegheny City.[205] Neither Lewis nor his brother Philipp Rinn are in the 1860 census. In 1870, their sister, Catharine, and her husband, Henry Peiker, and family lived in Allegheny City.[206]

Prior to his enrollment in Allegheny City in the Union Army on July 4, 1861, Lewis probably worked as a butcher and lived in Allegheny City. The next records for Lewis Rinn detail his Civil War military service.

Chapter 11

Lewis Rinn Going to War

Lewis Rinn left no recorded stories about his life as a soldier in the Civil War, but his military records confirm his service. What he likely experienced has been discovered from books and articles written about his regiment including letters and diaries written by his fellow soldiers in the 62nd Pennsylvania Voluntary Regiment, Infantry, Union Army.

Lewis Rinn Signed On

The American Civil War began on April 12, 1861, and Lewis Rinn enrolled at Allegheny City, Pennsylvania, in the Union Army on July 4, 1861. War fever moved people on that 4th of July as citizens lined the streets of Allegheny City waving American flags and shouting, "We'll show those damn rebels." People consumed plenty of food and beer while listening to speeches. Lewis must have felt one speaker talking to him when the orator raised his voice, pointed his finger, and shouted, "We need you young men to volunteer to save our country." Upon enrolling, Lewis described himself as being 5'10" with dark hair, blue eyes, and light complexion. At the age of 20, he committed to serve for three years.[207] However, it was unlikely he felt he would need to serve a three-year enlistment. Everyone in the North believed the South would be quickly defeated.

It is not known why Lewis Rinn enlisted. As a German immigrant, he may have felt the importance of

Muster-In Roll

preserving the Union. Most men did not join because they had a burning desire to stamp out slavery. Many joined because they wanted to take the defiant South and "set them straight." Others joined for a simpler reason—to take part in an exciting adventure or for the pay.[208]

For several weeks, notices had been posted around town to get volunteers. Colonel Sam Black, who was a leader from the Mexican American War, worked to recruit an Allegheny County regiment. The past few months, a group, including Lewis Rinn, drilled as a federal guard unit, formed by the Allegheny County Committee for Public Safety.[209] Not only was fighting a war quite an adventure for a young man, but the pay was $13 a month, worth approximately $367 in 2018 dollars.[210] Payments were to be made the 30th day of even-numbered months.

VOLUNTEERS WANTED
for
SCOTT LEGION Regiment

Col. S. W. Black
Late Col. of 1st Penn. Reg., Mexican War.

This regiment is accepted by the Secretary of War.

TO BE MUSTERED IN IMMEDIATELY

Head quarters,
Old Pennsylvania Bank,
Second Street, above Walnut.

Recruitment Notices

At first, Colonel Black's outfit was called the 33rd and came to be known as the 62nd Pennsylvania Voluntary Regiment, Infantry, Union Army. One of the earliest groups to sign up for a three-year term, Lewis Rinn's group of former federal guards became Company A.[211] The whole regiment was full within a week. Rinn enrolled as a private and reported to duty two and a half weeks later on July 22, 1861.[212]

The regiment recruits included city boys from Pittsburgh and Allegheny City, as well as farmers from surrounding areas. Some soldiers were immigrants, others were native born. The regiment originally had 1000 to 1200 men comprised of businessmen, ironworkers, glass blowers, boatmen, laborers, butchers, farmers, miners, and lumbermen. Company A originally had a Captain, a First and Second Lieutenant, five Sergeants, eight Corporals, and about seventy privates.[213]

Crowds Cheered

By August 1, 1861, Lewis Rinn and his regiment readied to leave the Pittsburg area. The unarmed soldiers, still in civilian dress, formed into line and moved out headed towards Pennsylvania Railroad Station. Enthusiastic civilians lined the streets as the regiment band played "The Girl I Left Behind Me." One member of the regiment later recalled "Thousands who assembled at the depot to take leave of us cheered us on with their approving smiles."[214]

On the 200-mile train trip across Pennsylvania to Harrisburg, citizens lined the rails, cheering and waving. The enthusiastic soldiers waved back. After two weeks drilling at Camp Cameron, the enthusiasm soon wore off. One soldier wrote home to his wife describing the daily drill routine: "The regiment woke at 5 a.m. and called roll, then it was squad drill from 6-7:30, company drill from 9:30-11, battalion drill from 4-6 p.m. and finally dress parade from 6-6:30. In between, the men found time to eat. At 9p.m. the drums beat to quarters, and lights out."[215]

On to Washington, DC

On August 19, the soldiers boarded a train and headed first to Baltimore and then Washington DC on their way to join the Army of the Potomac. Union supporters cheered the regiment that had climbed on and off trains, loaded and unloaded baggage, and pitched tents in three locations since leaving Pittsburgh. The young recruits watched in awe as other trains filled with soldiers, cannons, and ammunition moved into the city. Tents dotted every hill around Washington. Some estimated the assembled army to be between 150,000 to 180,000 soldiers.[216]

Lewis Rinn's regiment remained outside Washington DC defending the city and felling trees and constructing roads. The hot days and cold September nights took its toll on the men. Many soldiers took sick. They received their uniforms on September 3rd which consisted of a pair of sky-blue pantaloons and dark blue jacket, and hat. They were also issued a good overcoat, shoes, and underclothing.[217]

Union Army dress uniform (Library of Congress)

The uniformed regiment proudly marched through the capitol to the Arsenal where they got their arms and equipment. Some received Springfield rifles and others got the older muskets, the Enfield.

Fall 1861, Regiment Renamed

Tuesday, November 19, 1861, Lewis Rinn's regiment, the 33rd Pennsylvania Independent Regiment, became the 62nd Pennsylvania Volunteer Infantry as part of the Army of the Potomac.[218]

Regiment Drilled, Drilled, Drilled

In early October, the regiment moved near Falls Church, Virginia, and went into winter quarters. Colonel Black believed in enforcing drill and discipline to make his volunteers into a fighting unit, so they drilled, drilled and drilled until the parade ground in front of the camp was hard as a ball court from all the trampling. The constant drilling brought honor to the regiment when they won a silver cup on October 26 given to the best marching troop. One soldier recalled, "we marched past Gen. McClellan the first time slow and then went by him on double quick, and every man done his best."[219]

62nd Regiment Drilled (Library of Congress)

General George McClellan recognized the regiment's pursuit of excellence by giving them new uniforms. These fancy French Zouave outfits were supposed to be an honor. James L. Graham, a member of Company H wrote home describing the uniforms, "It is blue. The breeches are about three feet across the hips, tapering down to the ankle, a sort of blue monkey jacket, a large cape with a hood fastened to the back of it, one tight cloth skull cap with a tassel, and a dress parade cap which very much resembles our old patent leather cap. This cap has a plume of red, white, and blue feathers."[220]

Many soldiers, likely including Lewis Rinn, believed the uniforms were the ugliest on the banks of the Potomac. They felt like fools wearing the gaudy colored top and pants almost as full as a skirt. One soldier described the uniform as "a fancy one, with pants a man could carry 1 bushel of potatoes very handy in the seat of them."[221] Eventually, Colonel Black realized the uniform was impractical and ordered them packed up and sent back to Washington.

Zouave Uniform (Library of Congress)

Winter 1862, Winter of Inactivity-Mud, Filth, Disease

One of Lewis Rinn's fellow soldiers wrote:

We have been in winter camp near Falls Church, Virginia, since last October enduring the autumn chill and winter cold. There has been some snow and much rain which brought mud by mid-January. The camp streets turned into rivers of mud so we couldn't drill as much. Did you ever notice a fly endeavoring to walk through a dish of molasses? If you did, you can form some idea of why we can't march. Anyhow, I am sick and tired of drilling, review, and inspection.[222]

Soldiers had chores. Each day they cleaned tents, built pathways of pine logs, tended to horses, repaired equipment, gathered firewood, and hauled water. To safeguard the camp, they took turns standing guard duty.

At first, troops slept in circular tents made of linen and designed to hold 16 men side by side. These tents were 18 feet in diameter, with a center pole which contained a rack to hold weapons. In winter quarters, soldiers built rustic wooden cabins for protection from the weather. They chopped down trees and hauled them into camp. Then they set to work notching and laying the logs and filling the cracks with a mixture of wood chips and mud. Pine needles and leaves padded the bunks. To make themselves comfortable, the boys used whatever they had such as ammunition boxes for a table. Despite their best efforts, the huts soon sprang leaks and wind whistled through the cracks.[223]

Winter Quarters (Library of Congress)

The winter months brought camp fever (typhoid). Several soldiers died. Those that didn't die may have wished they had. At first, the camp was filthy beyond description. Every soldier was supposed to take a weekly bath, but some of the boys didn't bath that often. The lack of sanitation and hygiene attracted hordes of flies, mosquitoes, lice and fleas. The disease somewhat slowed after Surgeon James Kerr, introduced strict sanitary practices.[224]

Bad Food, Boredom & Entertainment

Food was not always good. Union soldiers sometimes had fresh meat, but some of the time troops got foul smelling salted meat that they soaked in water for several hours before it could be cooked. They fried the meat over the campfire in pans with globs of grease, which caused stomach problems. One doctor said he was having trouble preventing "death from the frying pan."[225]

During the winter, fresh vegetables were scarce. The army issued a strange concoction called, desiccated vegetables, a mixture of beans, onions, turnips, carrots, and beets—all dried and pressed into hard, bland cakes. To disguise the cakes, they were thrown into soup. One of the boys said that adding the cakes to liquid reminded him of a "dirty brook with all the dead leaves floating around." Flour and water crackers, called hardtack, were half-inch thick biscuits that were so hard that they called them "teeth dullers" or "sheet-iron crackers." Even worse, they often had worms and weevils.[226]

Soldiers tried to make the best of their dull winter camp routine by having some fun. Many a night, soldiers gathered around the campfire to sing. The favorite tunes were sentimental ballads— "Home Sweet Home," "Just Before the Battle, Mother," "The Girl I left Behind Me," and "When this Cruel War Is Over."[227]

There were strict rules against drinking liquor and gambling, but most of the officers gave up on enforcing restrictions against gambling. Soldiers risked money on everything—cards, dice games, cockfights, wrestling matches, baseball, and raffles.

Soldiers Gambled (Library of Congress)

Some young soldiers, away from home for the first time, took advantage of the new freedom by acting wild. The 62nd regiment had hard-workers and law abiders as well as rascals, scoundrels, shirkers, and outright thieves and pickpockets. There were the religious boys and the drinking boys and some who claimed to be both.[228]

After many months in winter camp, soldiers began to feel like caged animals. The huts that used to feel cozy, seemed crowded and stifling. Bunkmates, who once made others laugh with their pranks and jokes, seemed obnoxious and annoying. By spring of 1862, everyone wanted to get on with the business of war. Lewis Rinn probably thought, *"I am ready for the real business of war. I've been in this damn army for seven months and have yet to engage the enemy."*

Lewis Rinn on the Move, Summer 1862-The Battles Begin

On March 8, 1862, almost eight months after mustering in, Lewis Rinn and his regiment moved out of winter camp near Falls Church, Virginia. At the sound of the bugle at daybreak, the soldiers rolled up their blankets and prepared a meal. They loaded their backpacks with a blanket, a pair of socks, a piece of shelter tent, and three days' supply of food—bread, bacon and hardtack. They carried their rifles and a cartridge-box with 40 rounds. Stashed away in their backpacks was another 160 rounds of cartridges. On the 25-mile trip to Manassas, they marched at will with little semblance of military order singing, telling stories, and talking of the upcoming battle where they would lick the rebels. Troops did not stop for the noontime meal but ate as they marched.[229]

On March 10, the 62nd Regiment approached the enemy works at Manassas, also called Bull Run. But the rebels had withdrawn. They marched another 35 miles to Alexandria and became part of the Peninsula campaign. General McClellan planned to capture the Confederate capital of Richmond with the hope of a swift, war-winning victory.[230] After a march of more than 60 miles, Lewis Rinn probably was glad to board a transport headed for Yorktown, about 160 miles down the York River. For the transport of the entire Army of the Potomac from Washington to the peninsula, all manner of steamships and other vessels were commandeered. Some were large and comfortable; others were crowded and barely sea-worthy.[231]

Anxiety of First Battles-Peninsula Campaign

On April 3, 1862, the 62nd went into their first battle with the Confederate Army as they attacked Yorktown. Likely Lewis Rinn was both excited and afraid. One his fellow soldiers offered a last-minute prayer. His plea was, "Lord, if you ain't for us, don't be agin us. Just step aside and watch one of the worst fights you are likely to see."[232]

By the time the steady roll of drums signaled the regiment to advance, the suspense was almost unbearable. Troops moved forward under fire and took position in the line of battle. Months of drilling began to make sense. Soldiers marched elbow to elbow, keeping a distance of 13 inches from the person in front. When the order was given to fire, every other soldier was trained to shoot so that there was time to reload while the next soldier fired. It was awkward and tedious to reload as it took nine steps which included using their teeth to break open a cartridge containing a bullet and gunpowder.[233]

The siege of Yorktown lasted several weeks. One night, as the regiment held their position near the river, they saw three deserters come by with a white flag saying that the Confederates were evacuating Yorktown. The 62nd Regiment had won their first battle. Within minutes the American flag flew over Yorktown. Men of the 62nd celebrated with the bands playing the "Star Spangled Banner," "Hail Columbia," and other national airs. Cheers rang out as everyone chanted, "Yorktown has fallen."[234]

Fatigue from More Battles, More Defeats, More Marches

Later, both General Lee's army and General Stonewall Jackson's infantry attacked Lewis Rinn's regiment during the Seven Days' Campaign. One sharp battle after another took place as the Confederates tried to save their capital, Richmond, from being captured. Even though they were defeated, the leader of the 62nd Regiment, Colonel Black, proudly reported:

They went into action with their bodies broken by fatigue and their physical strength wasted by the hard toils of the day; but their spirits failed not, and they went in and came out with whatever credit is due to dangers bravely met and the noblest duty well performed.[235]

The Union Army gave up hope of capturing Richmond and retreated from the Peninsula. On August 14 the 62nd began a march of 60 miles in three days. In the heat of the warm, humid Virginia summer, this march was a killer. Their once pristine uniforms were stained, faded, rent and torn. Thank goodness for the sturdy army boots. To protect their feet, the troops thoroughly soaped their socks. They marched on to Newport News, where they immediately embarked on transports to leave the Peninsula.[236]

Summer 1862-First to Hear "Taps"

One warm summer evening, the Army of the Potomac first heard the new end-of-day bugle call. General Butterfield, one its commanders, wanted to honor the troops for their valiant efforts in the peninsular campaign. He didn't like the formal traditional army song that had been used. With the help of bugler, Oliver Norton, he composed a simple bugle call, which was called Taps—two short notes and one long. It soon caught on and everyone was playing Taps.[237]

Since leaving Pittsburgh the previous year, Lewis Rinn's regiment of slightly more than 1000 had lost 298 men killed, wounded, or missing—almost one third.[238] Lewis Rinn may have thought, "*What sights I have seen, what furious battles I have fought, yet to what end. I am tired of the real business of war.*" Some military historians blame Union Generals for attacking, retreating, and resting rather than fighting to win."[239]

Autumn 1862-The Bloodiest Day in American Combat History

On September 17th, the 62nd entered the Battle of Antietam near Sharpsburg, Maryland, where they supported a battery of 20 guns. All day, for 14 hours, both armies threw frontal attacks. The bloodiest day in American combat history ended with more than 23,000 casualties. Yet, they did no good. The battle ended in a draw.[240]

Battle Antietam, (Library of Congress)

Lewis Rinn likely saw the battlefield covered with bloodied bodies and heard the groans of dying men in all directions. The whole landscape turned red. The cornfield was so full of bodies that a man could have walked through it without stepping on the ground. As soon as the battle stopped, soldiers hunted for comrades, living and dead. Hundreds of craters pockmarked the ground from the ceaseless cannon and mortar fires. Bits and pieces of shattered trees, cannons, and wagons littered the earth. Frightened and wounded horses galloped over the landscape while wounded soldiers screamed for water or medical help. Each regiment had a suitable place for its dead. They put a headboard on each grave of those boys they could recognize.[241]

Such sights began to not affect the soldiers as they once did. War changed their sensitivities. Many soldiers knew they had been in the war too long when they looked at the body of a dead man as though they were looking at a dead horse or hog. Then they ate their meal, chatted with the boys, gambled and went to sleep.[242]

Dead Union and Confederate Soldiers at Antietam
(Library of Congress)

Defeated Again-Battle of Fredericksburg Trying to Take Hell

President Lincoln intended to sign the Emancipation Proclamation on New Year's Day 1863 and needed a military victory to silence his critics.[243] He pressured General Burnside to take Fredericksburg, Virginia. On December 13, 1862, the Army of the Potomac attacked General Lee and Stonewall Jackson. Thousands of casualties from both sides were scattered in the woods, marshes, and open fields near Fredericksburg. When President Lincoln heard that the Union Army lost the battle he moaned, *"If there is a place worse than hell, I'm in it!"* Though victorious, when General Lee observed the awful destruction, he whispered to James Longstreet, *"It is well that war is so terrible, or we would grow too fond of it."* One Union soldier said, *"We might as well have tried to take Hell."*[244]

Lewis Rinn's brothers, Phillip and Henry, as part of Pennsylvania's 123rd regiment, took part in the Battle of Fredericksburg too. Henry Rinn sustained a minor wound under his chin but survived.[245]

Lewis Rinn Reassigned-Left Frontline

Before Lewis Rinn enlisted, he was a butcher. In December 1862, he got the call to be detailed as a regiment butcher and went to the back line.[246] Some of the soldiers may have called him a "bombproof" because of his protected position, but he still worked hard serving his country.

Remembering Napoleon's quote, "The army marches on its' stomach,"[247] the commissary tried to give soldiers fresh meat or cured meat as often as possible. Union armies drove entire herds of cattle, pigs, and sheep behind the marching columns even while they were on campaign. Butchers traveled at the back of the marching units in the commissary wagons and often arrived at the campsites long after dark, sometimes at midnight.[248]

Army butchers slaughtered the animals and distributed uncooked meat to the troops for them to cook. The biggest problem during the Civil War was the inexperience of male army soldiers who did not know how to cook.[249] After a long day, soldiers gathered in small groups each evening to prepare their food. They called these groups "messes" and referred to others in the group as "messmates." Messmates took turns watching the meals they cooked. Food was cooked over an open campfire in a cast iron skillet or kettle or stove or occasionally on a spit. Before a march or battle, soldiers received a three-day allotment of their raw food and cooked it so they could carry it with them. A canvas haversack with a removable lining was used to carry food on the move. Although soldiers removed the lining and washed it when they had a chance, the haversacks soon smelled of old meat.[250]

Cooking Food

Curing salted beef or pork was another task performed by regiment butchers when the troops were not moving. Slabs of the heavy brined pork or beef were a stinky kind of blue meat that sometimes was a soldier's main supply of protein but not a favorite.[251]

Stuck in the Mud-the Mud March

Soon after Lewis Rinn became a regimental butcher, the army once again attempted to capture Richmond. A downpour of rain on January 21, 1863 made the roads impassable with troops, artillery, and wagons sunk in mud that grew deep, deep, and deeper. This unsuccessful campaign became known as Burnside's Mud March. Returning to camp was no easier moving backward than forward. Supplies and rations ran out. The boys were hungry and often shoeless, and dispirited. Finally, the army returned to winter camp near Falmouth, Virginia.[252] The winter of 1862-1863 was bitterly cold in Virginia. All night long the sounds of men coughing, breathing heavily, moaning and groaning could be heard.

April-June 1863-More Battles, More Defeats

Union troops headed towards Chancellorsville after having broken up winter quarters on April 27, 1863. At the front of the army was the 62nd Pennsylvania. The first Union force to see action, they exchanged skirmish fire with Confederate forces, and then were ordered to retreat, experiencing another defeat and Confederate victory.[253]

Sutler's Tent (Library of Congress)

May 1863, Lewis Rinn's regiment camped near Falmouth where the weather was hot and humid causing campsites to be dry and dusty. Sutlers, licensed traders, served the camp. Soldiers could buy extras such as pickles, cheese, sardines, cakes, candies, cigars, wine, beer, whiskey, pens, writing paper, needles and thread. The prices were outrageous, particularly after a payday that came every two months.[254]

1863-Chasing Lee to Gettysburg

By mid-June, rumors spread that the Confederate Army was on the move going north at breakneck speed towards Pennsylvania. The Army of the Potomac chased them, marching over 100 miles in five days with heavy rain much of the way. Some of the boys marched barefoot or in the remnants of their stockings. All were footsore and chafed and exhausted by the heat. On July 1, 1863, the 62nd regiment crossed into Pennsylvania. To speed up the pursuit, only four wagons accompanied the foot soldiers. Troops carried their own rations. Lewis Rinn and the commissary stayed behind. Troops struck out at 9 a.m. on a hot and stifling march to Gettysburg and into battle.[255]

At Gettysburg, the 62nd fought on the second day of battle. These brave men did not give up. In brutal hand-to-hand fighting and with many casualties after 12 hours of battle, they fought their way to safety. Later, a surviving soldier said death and havoc visited them that day. The regiment lost more soldiers in this battle than in any other, sustaining the highest loss of the brigade. Twenty-eight men were killed, 97 wounded. But their valiant efforts allowed a whole division of the Union Army to escape a trap set by the Confederates.[256]

When Lee retreated on July 5th, Lewis Rinn and the commissary rejoined the regiment as it marched south out of Gettysburg in pursuit of the withdrawing rebel army. One of the regiment soldiers said, *"Once more our now greatly decimated ranks are reformed and the column heads in the direction of the desolated hills and valleys of the now thoroughly despised and hated Virginia."*[257]

August 1863 to July 1864-the Battles Continue

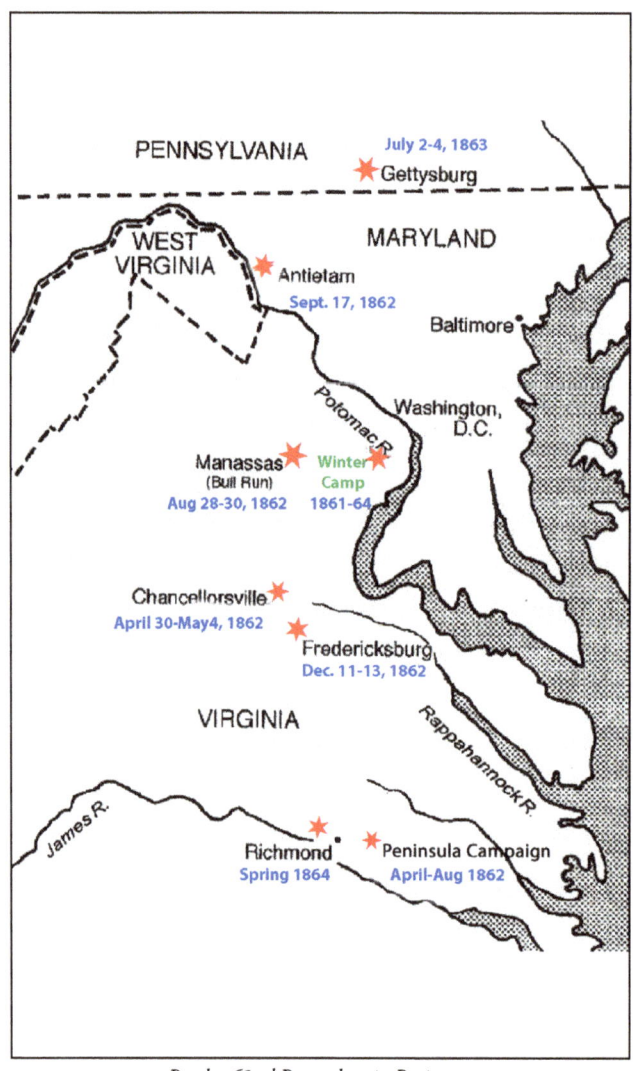

Battles-62nd Pennsylvania Regiment

After two years of service, soldiers of the 62nd regiment wanted to catch Lee, defeat him, and get the war over. Yet, their commanders held them back. Lee got away. President Lincoln said of the slow chase, "*The pursuit reminds me of an old woman trying to shoo her geese across a creek.*"[258]

The battles continued. Lewis Rinn's regiment patrolled the Rappahannock River until October and then participated in three months of battles in the Bristoe and Mine Run Campaigns. Winter of 1864 they had duty to patrol Bealeton Station, Virginia. All of May and part of June, they took more casualties in the Overland Campaign. They then moved on to the siege at Petersburg.[259]

July 1864-Heading Home at Last

Muster Out Image

Service for the 62nd Regiment ended in July, 1864, so they left the Petersburg battlefield on July 3rd. The war was not over, but they headed back home to Pittsburgh, Pennsylvania, to be mustered out. Lewis Rinn was lucky. He never thought he would need to serve three years, but he survived. His regiment was a fraction in size of what it once was. More than 56 percent of the men were killed, injured, or missing- 258 men were killed or died of disease, 503 wounded and 158 men captured or missing.[260]

The soldiers of the 62nd Pennsylvania Volunteer Infantry Regiment were brave, gallant, loyal, and well disciplined. During their three years of fighting, they achieved no special glory, lasting fame, nor particular distinction. They experienced both victories and defeats. Never did an action of the 62nd Pennsylvania create a decisive moment or a turning point in battle. They gained ground, held ground, and lost ground. They suffered severe casualties, particularly at Gaines Mills, Fredericksburg, Gettysburg, the Wilderness, and Spotsylvania. They marched, they waited,

Lewis Rinn Mustered Out

they carried out orders, they retreated. Twice orders they followed in battle were so controversial that the commanders giving them were either court-martialed or pressured to resign.[261] The soldiers fulfilled their duty.

On July 13, 1864 at Pittsburgh, Lewis Rinn mustered out of the Union Army and received pay $100 (approximately $1600 in 2018 money).[262] He had no more picket and guard duty, no more marching by day and night, no more camp life sleeping on the ground in all kinds of weather, no more danger of battle, sickness, and suffering from hunger and thirst. Lewis Rinn fulfilled his duty.

The German Bachelor & the French Girl

SUMMARY OF LEWIS RINN'S CIVIL WAR SERVICE		
July 4, 1861	Allegheny City, Pennsylvania	**Private Lewis Rinn mustered in.**
July 24 1861	Pittsburgh to Harrisburg	Marched out of Pittsburgh.
August 3, 1861	Harrisburg, Pennsylvania	Received instruction in drilling.
August 17th-27th, 1861	Baltimore, Maryland	Traveled.
August 28, 1861	Washington, D.C.	Camped outside city.
September 3, 1861	Washington, D.C.	Received uniforms.
September 4th, 1861	Washington D.C.	Marched to arsenal to get rifles.
September 8th, 1861	Fort Corcoran, Virginia	Duty to defend Washington D.C.
Octoober, 1861	Falls Church, Virginia	Went into winter camp for drilling.

1862		
March 8-10, 1862	Manassas, Virginia	25-mile march to find enemy withdrawn.
March 10, 1862	Alexandria, Virginia	35-mile march.
Part of the Peninsula campaign.		
March 22, 1862	Yorktown, Virginia	Did reconnaissance work.
April 3, 1862	Yorktown, Virginia	Attacked Yorktown for several weeks.

CONFEDERATES EVACUATED YORKTOWN		
June 26, 1862	Yorktown, Virginia	Seven Day's Campaign. Defeated by General Lee and General Jackson.
June 27, 1862	West Point, Virginia	Won Battle of Gaines Mill.
June 28-30, 1862	Near Glendale, Virginia	Won Battle of Malvern Hill.
July-August, 1862	Harrison Landing,	VirginiaCamped for six weeks.
August 14, 1862	Newport News, Virginia	Marched sixty miles in three days.
August 1862	Manassas, Virginia	Remained in reserve at second Bull Run.
September 1862	Falls Church, Virginia	Rested.
September 17, 1862	Sharpsburg, Maryland	Battle of Antietam was a draw with 23,000 casualties.
December 1862	Fredericksburg, Virginia	Battle of Fredericksburg was Confederate victory.
December 1862	Virginia	Lewis Rinn detailed as regiment butcher for duration of service.

1863		
January 21, 1863	Rappahannock River, Virginia	Mud March bogged down.
January 24-April 27, 1863	Falmouth, Virginia	Went into winter camp.
April 27, 1863	Chancellor, Virginia	Battle of Chancellor.
May-July 1863	Falmouth, Virginia	Rested at camp.
Mid-June-July 5, 1863	Virginia to Gettysburg	Forced march of 100 miles in five days.
July 3, 1863	Gettysburg, Pennsylvania	Engaged in last day of battle.
July 5-24, 1863	Gettysburg to Virginia	Pursed Confederates back to Virginia.
October-December 1863	Rappahannock River, Virginia	Battles of Bristoe and Mine Run

1864		
Winter 1864	Bealeton Station, Virginia	Patrol duty.
May-June 1864	James River, Virginia	Overland Campaign battles.
July 1864	Petersburg, Virginia	Part of the siege until July 3. Left battlefield.
July 13, 1864	Pittsburgh, Pennsylvania	**Private Lewis Rinn mustered out**

Chapter 12

Lewis Rinn Moving West

First Back Home to Pennsylvania

After mustering out of the Union Army on July 13, 1864, Lewis Rinn returned home to Allegheny City, Pennsylvania. He rejoined his older brother, Jacob, and sister, Catherine Elizabeth, and their families as well as brothers Philipp and Henry who had returned home before him on May 31, 1864, at the completion of their one-year enlistment in Pennsylvania's 123rd regiment. His mother, Anna Marie Rinn, had died in 1852 and was buried in Saint Paul's Cemetery there. No records have been located for his father, Ludwig Rinn, Sr.[263]

The Pittsburgh area thrived during and after the war. It produced over one-half of all domestic steel and more than one-third of all U.S. glass. It's location on the confluence of the Monongahela, Allegheny and Ohio rivers made it an important transportation hub.[264] Between 1860-1870 the city of Pittsburgh grew from about 50,000 to 86,000 people with a strong influx of German immigrants.[265] Lewis Rinn stated in his Civil War pension application in 1893 that after the war, he resided in Pennsylvania, Missouri and Indian Territory.[266] He provided no dates.

Migrated to Missouri

Mass migration to the Midwest followed the end of the Civil War. Previously, the area had a relatively tiny population. The establishment of rule of law, expansion of railroads, and the implementation of the Homestead Act of 1862 attracted people, especially German Americans.[267]

Lewis Rinn and his younger brother, Henry, joined in this migration as they traveled the 600 miles from Pittsburgh to St. Louis. Their mode of transportation and exact date is not known, but it is possible they took the train. The Pittsburgh to St. Louis Main Line, operated by the Pennsylvania Railroad, ran west from Pittsburgh in 1865, to Steubenville, Columbus, and Dayton, Ohio, then to Indianapolis and Terre Haute, Indiana, and finally to Vandalia and East St. Louis, Illinois.[268] Likely they crossed the Mississippi River to St. Louis, Missouri, by ferry because the Eads Bridge was not completed until July 4, 1874.[269]

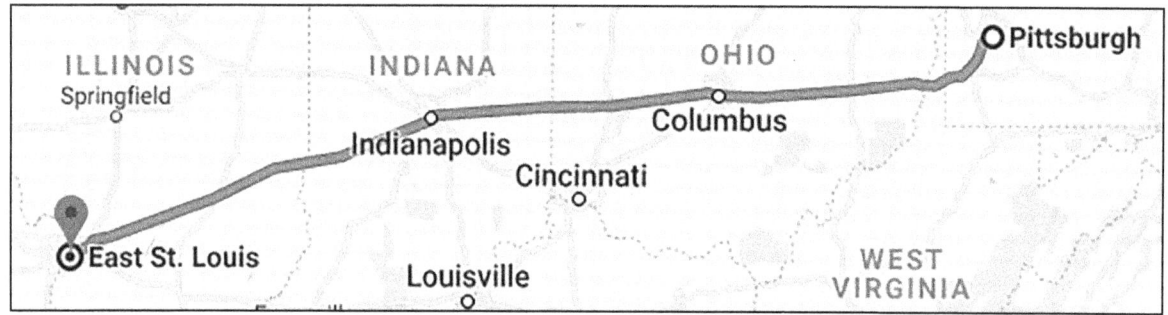
Pittsburgh to East St. Louis

When the Rinn brothers reached St. Louis, they found a thriving, growing city with a large German population. St. Louis grew after the Civil War when migration, immigration, and industrialization sparked a significant population boom. The population expanded from 160,000 people in 1860 to over 310,000 by 1870.[270]

Lewis Rinn's brother, Henry, settled in St. Louis, married German immigrant Anna Marie Osten in1867, raised a large family, and owned a butcher shop.[271]

While in St. Louis, Lewis had his picture taken. The photo shows a handsome young man likely in his 20s with abundant dark hair and blue eyes. A trimmed mustache accents his light complexioned face. He stood about 5'10" and wore a dress coat and plaid dress pants.

Lewis Rinn, Picture taken in St. Louis About 1865-1868

Moved on to Indian Territory

Bachelor Lewis Rinn decided to leave Missouri and traveled almost 600 miles south and west to Indian Territory. In 1834, the U.S. government had set aside an area for Native Americans called Indian Territory in Kansas, Nebraska, and Oklahoma north and east of the Red River. In 1854, Kansas and Nebraska were re-designated territories open to white settlement. The Indian Territory that Rinn went to was western Oklahoma.[272]

Supplied Meat to Camp Supply

Lewis Rinn was living at Camp Supply, Indian Territory, in 1876.[273] As a civilian butcher, he supplied meat to the army.[274]

Originally called Camp Supply and then named Fort Supply, the remote fort was located in western Oklahoma in present day Woodward County. The nearest settlement was Dodge City, Kansas, almost 100 miles away. The post served as a supply point for troops who acted as peace keepers for the Cheyenne and Arapaho reservation and the Cherokee Outlet. Cavalry also escorted cattle drives along the Texas Trail as they made their way through the territory from Texas to Dodge City, Kansas. Later, in 1879, the soldiers were ordered to expel boomers illegally entering the Cherokee Outlet.[275]

Early in the summer of 1876, 34-year-old bachelor Lewis Rinn, lived in a boarding house near the fort. There he met the vivacious French girl, Marguerite Clair, and his life changed forever.

Part IV

The Spirited Bunch
Lewis and Marguerite's Children

"Mama and Papa had ten children and nine of us lived to be adults. Sometimes we fought, but mostly we loved one another."

~Jessie Rinn, youngest daughter

Family of Lewis and Marguerite Clair Rinn

Lewis Rinn
1841-1905

Marguerite Clair
1857-1919

Ten Children

Lottie Rinn
1877-1920

Claire Rinn   1879-1962

Claude Rinn
1881-1974

Violet Rinn
1883-1955

Theoda Rinn
1885-1958

Lewis Rinn
1887-1973

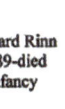

Edward Rinn
1889-died
infancy

Edmond Rinn
1891-1967

Seona Rinn
1893-1984

Jessie Rinn
1896-1992

Chapter 13

LOTTIE BENOITE RINN
1877-1920

Young Lottie

BORN IN INDIAN TERRITORY

A short ten months after Lewis and Marguerite married, the birth of Lottie Benoite Rinn on May 30, 1877 at Camp Supply in Indian Territory started their large family. Eventually, Lottie had three brothers and five sisters. In 1882, when she was about five years old, the family moved 330 miles east to Franklin County, Kansas, near the town of Williamsburg. Her maternal grandmother, Benoite Clair, lived there. Her family initially lived on the Clair property at the Silkville commune where Marguerite's family settled in 1869. Lottie may have attended the Silkville school which opened in 1881. Soon the family moved into Williamsburg which was about two miles away. Her father ran a meat market and her mother had a restaurant/ice cream store. She likely attended school in Williamsburg through eighth grade. No doubt, Lottie helped with the housework and the younger children, too.

Worked in Ottawa But Visited Family and Friends

By 1900, 23-year-old Lottie worked in the household of L.C. Stine in Ottawa, Kansas. Mr. Stine, president of the bank, was an important local businessman in Ottawa and Williamsburg. After he influenced De Boissiere to give Silkville to the Odd Fellow organization, Stine became Superintendent of the Orphans home at Silkville. Lottie helped take care of the household that included Mr. and Mrs. Stine, their adult son and high school aged daughter, plus a boarder who was a college student. Ottawa was about 15 miles from Williamsburg. The Williamsburg newspaper reported her frequent visits home and the trips that her sister, Claire, made to Ottawa to visit Lottie. One summer, Lottie went to Colorado to visit a friend. At other times, she traveled to Baldwin, Kansas, to visit her grandmother Clair and her aunt's Jardon family. All her traveling was done by train.

Followed Family to Oklahoma

When the Rinns left Kansas in the fall of 1901 to resettle in Oklahoma, Lottie, along with her sister, Claire, remained in Kansas until the Rinns were settled, at which time the sisters joined the family in the Spring of 1902. Sister, Jessie Rinn, in an interview in the 1990s, stated that Lottie and Claire went to El Reno about 30 miles away and got jobs with Lottie working for Singer Sewing Machine Company. It is believed that Lottie was an accomplished seamstress and cook. She had an ornate silver thimble and some fancy hand painted German plates that remain in the family.

Lottie and Frank Pond on Colorado Honeymoon

Married Francis (Frank) Pond and Traveled the Country

It was in El Reno that Lottie met Frank Pond, a tall, handsome, blue eyed, stockman, born in Illinois. Nine years Lottie's senior, Frank had recently obtained a divorce from his first wife. Although married about 10 years, he had no children. At age 28, Lottie received an attractive emerald and diamond engagement ring. On January 5, 1906 Frank and Lottie traveled to Fort Worth, Texas, to be married by the Justice of the Peace. The couple made their first home in El Reno and later moved nearer the Rinn homeplace in Grady County.

Ponds and Martins
1906 Honeymoon in Colorado

MOTHER OF FOUR SONS

While they lived in Oklahoma, Lottie gave birth to Donald Clifford Pond on October 22, 1906, and to Francis Lewis "Frank" Pond on July 24, 1908. About this time, Frank received an inheritance from his family who lived in Menard County, Illinois. The Pond family set out traveling. They were living in Eugene, Oregon, for Eugene Claire "Gene" Pond's birth on March 31, 1910. Sometime afterwards the family moved to Florida. Gene Pond always told the story that he learned to swim there when his older brothers threw him into the alligator infested waters. Although the Pond family enjoyed their travels across the country from Oregon to Florida, Lottie always missed her Rinn family. On Thanksgiving of 1915, Lottie sent a card to her sister, Theoda, in Oklahoma, saying she missed the family. Later, living in Missouri, Lottie sent letters to her mother saying she missed her and wanted her to visit.

Ponds in Kansas 1919
FR: Gene, Tom, BR: Frank Sr., Don, Lottie, Frank Jr.

By 1916 when Thomas Russell "Tom" Pond was born, the Ponds were back in Oklahoma living on a farm south of Chickasha. Later Theoda Rinn Martin stated in a delayed birth record that she was present at the birth of Tom. Sometime before 1920 the Ponds moved to Neodesha, Kansas. where Frank worked in the oil refineries. They lived on Ohio Street. Gene Pond used to tell the story that during a tornado in Kansas he saw a church turn around on its foundation.

Lottie Died

In the fall of 1920, 42-year-old Lottie suffered a miscarriage. In spite of three weeks of medical treatment, she developed peritonitis and died on October 25, 1920. She is buried at the Mount Hope Cemetery in Independence, Kansas, about 20 miles from Neodesha. The Rinns were devastated when they received the news. Jessie Rinn kept a calendar all her life with the day after Lottie's death circled. It was the day she got word of Lottie's death. It is believed that Jessie, her mother Marguerite, and others traveled to Neodesha to comfort the Ponds, especially Lottie's four boys who were 14, 12, 10 and 4.

Youngest Sons Lived with Grandma Rinn

The family was concerned about the boys. It was decided that the older two sons, Don and Frank, would remain with their dad in Kansas. Ten-year-old Gene and four-year-old Tom came down to Oklahoma to live on the Rinn farm with their grandmother Rinn and Aunt Jessie. Aunt Theoda's family lived in a separate house on the farm so the boys played with their cousins, Marguerite and Louise Martin, and attended the Hazel Dell School. They were surrounded by their loving Rinn aunts and uncles. When Edmund and Susie Rinn had their second son, they named him Gene, after Gene Pond. This must have meant something to a young boy who had lost his mother. Tom was a very cute and charming little boy. His grandmother and

Picture of Pond boys likely taken at Lottie's funeral. FR: Gene, Tom, BR: Don & Frank

Aunt Jessie loved to spoil him and dress him up for special programs at school. It was at school that Gene met a neighbor, Hazel Chappell, in third grade. Eventually, a school romance developed which later led to marriage.

Gene Pond recalled that his grandmother was an excellent cook. He told about her mincemeat curing in the cellar. The Rinn cousins liked to sneak down there and take a taste of the heady mixture. He remembered his aunts getting on the country line telephone and talking in French just to annoy their neighbors who liked to listen in.

Ponds Moved to California

Sometime in 1923, Frank Pond gathered up his boys and moved to California. They traveled by car. When they came to the desert at Yuma, Arizona, they drove across the sand dunes on a wooden plank road. The family first settled in El Segundo along the southern California coast. Gene Pond remembered diving off the pier at El Segundo and swimming to Manhattan Beach, a distance of two plus miles. Father, Frank, had remarried, and so the boys had a stepmother and two stepsisters. Later, the family moved inland to a small acreage west of Ontario, California, where Frank had a chicken ranch and his wife, Fannie, ran a restaurant..

Lottie's Sons

Lottie's sons were handsome, smart and ambitious. They believed that if they tried hard enough, they could do anything.

Donald Clifford Pond (1906-1976) The oldest Rinn grandchild was born October 22, 1906 in El Reno, Canadian County, Oklahoma. He was 14 when his mother died. When his family moved to California, he was 17 and attended barber college in Los Angeles. In 1940 when he filled out a draft card for WWII, he said he was 6' tall, weighed 155 pounds, had blue eyes and brownish-red hair. He enlisted in the army as a private on August 10, 1942. After the war, he moved to Rodeo, California, where he established a barbershop. In 1948, he married Elaine Skinner. They had no children. Later, Don worked in real estate when they lived in Pinole, California. He developed emphysema and lung cancer and passed away at the age of 69 in April 1976. He is buried at Ainsworth, Nebraska, his wife's hometown.

Francis Lewis "Frank" Pond (1908-1977) was born July 24, 1908 in Oklahoma. Twelve when his mother died, he completed high school in Kansas and went to barber college in Los Angeles. As a young man, Frank married Margarete McComber and had a son born in April 1929, who lived in Los Angeles, later taking the last name of his stepfather, Whitinghill. Frank enlisted in the Army as a private on March 15, 1943, and was discharged October 10, 1945. At the time of his enlistment, he said he was employed as a hotel manager, was 5'11," had blue eyes and brown hair.

After the war, Frank became manager of a resort in Coarsegold, California, near Yosemite National Park. He married Helen Lindsey. The couple had no children. Later, they moved to Huntington Beach, California, where Frank worked for Douglas Aircraft Company until retirement. He developed lung disease and passed away at the age of 69 on October 24, 1977 in Huntington Beach, California.

Eugene Claire "Gene" Pond (1910-1970) was born March 31, 1910 in Eugene, Oregon. He was 10 when his mother died. For several years, he and his younger brother, Tom, lived with his grandmother Rinn and attended Hazel Dell school before moving to California. He never forgot his first girlfriend, Hazel Chappell, in Oklahoma. Over the years, he and his Dad made trips back to Oklahoma where Gene would visit Hazel Chappell. In 1933 Gene returned to Oklahoma and lived with Ruel and Seona Rinn Daggs on a farm west of Minco. He always had fond memories of living there with his Aunt Seona and family. Gene courted Hazel Chappell. They married on October 6, 1934, in Kingfisher, Oklahoma, with cousin, Marguerite Martin Pinkston and her husband, Tommy, as witnesses. The first year of marriage, Hazel and Gene lived near Chickasha and gathered at Aunt Jessie's on Friday nights to play Pitch with the family.

The couple moved to Ontario, California, in December 1935. In 1937 they moved to Fullerton where their twin daughters were born. Later they moved to Santa Ana where Gene opened Gene's Floorcovering store in 1941. Initially, the work involved installing floorcovering for the Santa Ana Air Base. After the war, it became a successful business for the next 20 years.

Gene Pond always had a lot of confidence and thought he could do anything. He was short—about five foot five, with large blue eyes and the Rinn hooked nose. Family was important to him. He encouraged his daughters to get an education. When they went away to college he said, "If you don't like it there, I will trade with you."

Gene Pond developed lung disease and passed away at the age of 59 on February 18, 1970. He is buried at Fairhaven Cemetery, Santa Ana, California.

Thomas Russell "Tom" Pond (1916-1984) was born May 3, 1916 in Minco, Oklahoma.

He was four when his mother died. Along with Gene, he lived with his grandmother Rinn and attended Hazel Dell school before moving to California. He attended school in Ontario, California. Later as a teenager, he lived in Enid, Oklahoma, likely with his uncle Claude Rinn, where he learned the grocery business. Sometime after 1935, he returned to Los Angeles and worked first as a clerk and then manager of grocery stores. On his WWII Draft registration card, he described himself being 5'7" weighing 147 pounds and having blue eyes, and brown hair. He married Louella Christman in 1941 and had two sons. Later he divorced and married Margaret Ilsley in 1947 and had nine children. They lived in Torrance, California, where the entire family worked in the grocery business.

Like his brothers, Tom developed lung disease. After a series of strokes, he passed away at the age of 68 on December 21, 1984, in Torrance, California

Pond Brothers 1940s. from L-R: Don, Tom, Frank, Gene

Chapter 14

CLAIRE LOUISE RINN

1879-1962

Young Claire

CONTRIBUTED BY THE LATE PAULA PHILLIPS, GRANDDAUGHTER

Born December 2, 1879 at Camp Supply, Indian Territory, Claire Louise Rinn, the next to the oldest of the Rinn children, was unlike her siblings. She was a tiny, shy woman, less than five feet tall and never weighing so much as a 100 pounds. She grew up in Williamsburg, Kansas, where she knew Ralph Waldo Fultz. When her parents moved to Oklahoma, she and her older sister, Lottie, initially stayed in Kansas until the family was settled and then they came to Oklahoma. After moving, she had a job in El Reno.

Married

On January 10, 1906, at the age of 27, she married Ralph Fultz. Her only child, Pauline Claire Fultz, was born on December 10, 1906. The Fultz family moved back and forth between Arkansas City, Kansas, and Newkirk, Oklahoma.

Although Ralph was well liked by many of the Rinn clan, the marriage was troubled as a consequence of his health problems resulting from a poorly healed broken leg and abuse of prescription medication given for the pain.

Ralph & Claire Fultz

Eventually Claire felt she had no alternative to divorce, an action almost unheard of at the time. Employment opportunities for women were very limited so Claire supported herself and Pauline by milking cows and doing other grueling work in a Kansas dairy. During this period, her life was essentially a struggle for survival.

Remarried

When Pauline was still in elementary school, on March 8, 1916, Claire married widower Everett V. "Eb" Cole, whose first wife was Anna Martin, sister to Will Martin who was married to Claire's sister Theoda. No doubt, the family introduced the couple.

Following the marriage, Claire, Pauline, "Eb," and his daughter, Gladys, settled on a farm outside of Minco. A stern, demanding man, Eb was a good provider and a very

Pauline & Claire Fultz about 1911

successful farmer. Their large farm home, painted dark green with white trim, was the scene of many wonderful Rinn family get-togethers. On some holidays, from 50 to 75 people would gather to enjoy the wonderful cooking of the Rinn sisters. The men would eat at the first sitting, then the children, and finally the women would eat what was left. The sisters spent the rest of the afternoon in the kitchen cleaning up and chattering in French.

The Rinn sisters also used their French to circumvent the listeners on the multi-party telephone lines. Entertainment being somewhat limited, people commonly picked up and listened to calls of others. The sisters would laugh and say that, when they switched to French, receivers would begin clicking all along the line.

WORKED HARD

Tiny Claire worked as hard as a field hand. She regularly began her day at 4:00 a.m. when she would prepare the separator and begin running the milk from the large dairy herd through it; then she would wash all of the equipment to repeat the same process in the late afternoon. She tended a large flock of chickens, gathered and cleaned the eggs before boxing them in the cellar for delivery to town. Eggs and cream were sold weekly in Minco. The skim milk was fed to Eb's Red Durrock hogs. Claire made a large garden, canning and preserving the produce for the year's provisions. In those days before freezers or locker plants, she even canned the sausage and other pork which was not cured in the smoke house. Chicken and pork were the primary meats in their diet. When beef was butchered, usually several families would go in together and take a quarter each. Of course, she made all of their bread. The Cole's orchard provided apples, apricots, cherries, peaches, and plums eaten fresh in season and canned for later use. Some fruits, especially plums, cherries, and grapes, were canned as juice for jellies.

During harvest time, Claire cooked massive noon meals for the field workers. Usually there would be at least two large cookie sheets of homemade rolls, three or four pies, a couple of cakes, a meat course, and countless vegetables.

Laundry was done weekly in water heated on a wood stove in the wash house. Ironing was with heavy flat irons heated on the wood stove. In addition to all of this backbreaking labor, Claire kept an immaculate house, even dusting upstairs and downstairs window sills weekly. Her reputation as a housekeeper was such that sisters and sisters-in-law would say things like, "Oh, Claire's coming. I've got to get busy and polish the silver."

Claire's only respite from farm labor was her exquisite hand work. Besides making all of the family clothes, including Eb's shirts, she did fine embroidery and created countless quilts, many of which have been preserved and cherished by her descendants. Her favorite quilt patterns were the Double Wedding Ring and the Flower Garden.

For several years, Claire also found time to write letters to her mother's family in Saint Etienne, France. She kept a collection of French letters dating until the late 1930s from the Gonon family. Unfortunately, they were discarded.

Moved to Chickasha

When Eb and Claire were in their seventies, they sold the farm and moved to a small house in Chickasha, not far from Claire's brother Edmond and his wife, Susie. Eb was a dominant and controlling force in Claire's life. When he died in October 1952, Claire had never been to the grocery store alone, did not know how to write a check, and could not drive a car. Timid, often terrified alone, Claire could not cope with Twentieth Century life.

Relocated Near Daughter in Arkansas

Eventually, Pauline moved her to Russellville, Arkansas, in a small house next door to her own home. Claire remained there until it was necessary for her to be in a nursing home. She died at the age of 83 on June 22, 1962. She is buried in Evergreen Cemetery in Minco, Oklahoma near many of her siblings.

Daughter

Pauline Claire Fultz (1906-1998) the oldest Rinn granddaughter, was born December 10, 1906, in Newkirk, Oklahoma. A spunky, extroverted, freckle-faced redhead, she was almost the antithesis of her mother, Claire. The only similarity between the two was their petite stature. Growing up, Pauline liked riding horses, climbing trees, playing baseball—anything active and outdoors.

Mischief at Minco High School

Because the Cole family, Claire, Eb, his daughter Gladys, and Pauline, lived about 10 miles from town in the era before school buses, to attend high school Pauline had to board during the week in Minco. Pauline and her cousin Marguerite Martin were roommates at Mrs. Grant's boarding house. What mischief one did not think up the other did. The school superintendent, Prof Perry as they referred to him, labeled the two "The Katzenjammers." If they were returning late to the boarding house from whatever they could find to do in Minco, they would scare Mrs. Grant's chickens. When she went out to see what was after her chickens, the girls would sneak in and rush up to their room.

Pauline Fultz, about 20

Escaped to Muskogee, Oklahoma

Pauline had a mind of her own. Upon high school graduation, her stepfather decided she would teach school because all that was required to teach at that time was a high school diploma and satisfactory completion of the "teacher's test." On the test, she deliberately answered incorrectly as many questions as she dared, but she was given a teacher's certificate anyhow. She told her stepfather that she would not teach school. He said, "You are teaching school."

Pauline, in secret, turned to her Grandma, Marguerite Rinn. She begged her grandmother to help, pleading, "Did you ever make your kids do what they absolutely hated?" Grandma Rinn gave Pauline 10 dollars to finance her escape. When the Cole family went to Minco the next Saturday, Pauline feigned illness and stayed home. As soon as the family was out of sight, with a few belongings and her 10 dollars, she persuaded a neighbor boy to take her to Pocasset, where she caught a train to Muskogee where one of her father's relatives lived. Pauline got a job as a telephone operator where she worked a split shift and attended Draughns Business College between shifts. After polishing her business skills, Pauline worked in a bank in Muskogee.

Married

In 1930, she married a career soldier, Joseph R. "Jimmie" Phillips. Marriage to a career soldier was not easy, but Pauline was a born survivor. Two daughters were born. During the years of World War II, the couple lived in numerous states. Upon Jimmie's retirement, the family relocated to Russellville, Arkansas, where her girls finished school. Pauline went to work as a bookkeeper/secretary for Cogswell Motors where she worked until her retirement at age 72.

Pauline's life centered around work and family. She had no hobbies, was neither a joiner nor a church goer. Always impeccably groomed, she is remembered variously as being cute, feisty, prissy. The most rancorous disagreement between Pauline and her daughter occurred when her daughter insisted that Pauline, in her eighties, give up her trademark spike-heeled shoes. Even in the nursing home after a series of strokes, nearing age 90, when complimented on how pretty she looked, Pauline would reply, "I haven't looked like anything since my daughter took away my high-heeled shoes."

Pauline Fultz Phillips died of pneumonia at the age of 92 February 03, 1998 in Russellville, Arkansas. She is buried near her aunts and mother in Evergreen Cemetery, Minco, Oklahoma.

Chapter 15

DANIEL CLAUDE RINN
1881-1956

Young Claude

CONTRIBUTED BY THE LATE R. SCOTT RINN, GRANDSON

Lewis and Marguerite Rinn announced the birth of Daniel Claude, on October 1, 1881, at Camp Supply in Indian Territory. Daniel Claude was the third of nine children. He was two years old when the family moved to Williamsburg, Kansas. He grew up in this small town of about 800 people which was located south of Ottawa. Although the family called him "Claude" after Marguerite's father, he was known as Daniel or Dan at school and in town.

GREW UP IN WILLIAMSBURG, KANSAS

He attended school in Williamsburg. After completing his eighth-grade education, it is assumed he worked in his Dad's butcher shop and helped his Mother with her ice cream store and restaurant. In the summer of 1900 when he was 19, the Williamsburg newspaper reported that Dan Rinn was working for William Bitts on a farm west of Williamsburg. The Bitts were friends of the Rinns with a long acquaintance going back to the days when the Bitts worked at Silkville when Marguerite was growing up. Not all was work, because the same newspaper reported that on August 10, 1900, Dan Rinn went to the show in Ottawa.

Like many of his siblings, Daniel Claude, exhibited a strong, independent personality, a virulent strain of prairie humor and a good dose of common sense. All the Rinn children spoke French in the house until they attended school so they could communicate with their French speaking grandmother, Benoite Clair.

According to the March 22, 1901 edition of the Williamsburg Star newspaper, Daniel and Violet Rinn were initiated into the Knights and Ladies Security where their parents belonged. This organization was a fraternal and benevolent society that extended life insurance to its members. It was also a social organization that met on the first and third Wednesday evenings in Williamsburg.

It is known that Claude, along with older sisters Lottie and Claire, stayed behind when the family left Williamsburg on October 29, 1901 to move to Oklahoma. Apparently, Claude had a job. After the Rinns left for Oklahoma, it was reported in the Williamsburg Republican Newspaper on November 2, 1901 that Dan Rinn was assisting in the Northside Meat Market, his father's old butcher shop.

MOVED TO OKLAHOMA

When the Rinns arrived in Oklahoma and completed work on their house, Claude, as the oldest boy, was given the job of packing up the family's furniture and gathering its cattle to put on the Rock Island Railroad to Indian Territory. The railroad had extended its tracks in 1890 from the Cherokee Outlet to Minco, located just east of the land Lewis won by lottery in the former Wichita Indian Reservation just south of the Canadian River. It was a beautiful 160-acre tract of land containing a creek lined on either side by shade trees. Claude arranged for a large wagon at the Minco station to drive the family's belongings out to their new home.

During this first winter in Indian Territory, Claude was 20 years old and itching to strike out on his own. He had an eighth grade education and the determination to make something of himself. Like the children of many immigrants, Claude avoided the French and German languages spoken by his parents, but he knew French because it was the language of his mother. While Claude's relationship with his parents is unknown, there is a story that Lewis kicked Claude out of the house on one occasion for sassing his mother. Though Claude returned to his parents' good graces, he probably kept a sharp lookout for an opportunity that would allow him to leave the farm for a future all his own. He was 5'8", brown eyed, with brown hair, ruddy complexion.

Claude had two brothers and six sisters, who would, to the annoyance of an enamored sibling, revert to French for purposes of gossiping in front of suitors who would visit the house. Claude was noted for giving a strong handshake. His youngest sister, Jessie, recalled that her boyfriends were greeted by Claude who grabbed their hand and grasped it until they gave up. Nephew, Don Daggs, recalled years later his uncle giving him the robust handshake.

LEFT HOME TO WORK ON RAILROAD

He had been fascinated by the railroad operations he experienced while bringing the family belongings by freight train to Minco and it wasn't long before Claude landed a job with the Rock Island Railroad as a switchman. He became familiar with the various stations where the Rock Island stopped on its route from Kansas, through Indian Territory and on to Texas. He decided after a time, however, that what he really wanted was to start his own business. He had stopped in Enid on a number of occasions and liked what he saw of the town's spirit and the business opportunities he believed existed in one of Oklahoma's fastest growing cities.

SETTLED IN ENID, OKLAHOMA

In 1905, when Claude Rinn left his job as a switchman on the Rock Island Railroad, he decided to take a job as a butcher in the railroad-owned grocery store located in Enid. The nomadic railroad life did not offer Claude the business prospects he wanted. He had apprenticed as a butcher for many years at the side of his father, Lewis, and applied himself to his new job, rapidly gaining a reputation as one of Enid's top butchers.

When Claude arrived in Enid, the town had grown to 12,123. This area was still not a state, and maintained its status as a Territory until 1907 when Oklahoma became the country's 46th state the following year. For most Enidites, the biggest difference between living in a Territory and living in a State was how they bought their liquor. Oklahoma entered the union as a "dry" state on November 16, 1907 and the bootlegging of moonshine began on November 17th. In Enid, 25 saloons around the downtown square went out of business overnight.

Claude became a successful businessman

Enid was a tough, hard working town run by Republican businessmen in a state dominated by the Democrat party. It was the third largest city in the new state of Oklahoma, and was described in a St. Louis editorial as "a rattling good city ... aggressive ... distinguished as being about the only one of the larger towns of Oklahoma or Indian Territory which does not aspire to be the state capitol." Claude was in the middle of everything to do about Enid. He was a "man about town." He ran a thriving grocery business and joined any number of civic organizations. In later years, one of Claude Rinn's neighbors in Enid laughingly described him as a "banny rooster," an aggressive man who would embrace a challenge – a man you could count on to get things done.

Married Anna Reeves

In 1908, at the age of 27, Claude met 22-year-old Anna Mabel Reeves, a young woman selling millenary products for a company headquartered in Kansas City. Part of Anna's territory included Enid. On one occasion she met the proprietor of the Rinn grocery store. Claude was immediately impressed with this smart-looking young woman from Missouri and, largely ignoring the products she was selling, went to work selling her on the idea of marriage. Anna's family came to Missouri from Iowa. Anna was raised on a farm in Braymer, Missouri, northeast of Kansas City by her mother and older siblings.

Anna and Claude each had a natural instinct for business. Both had Civil War veterans for fathers, each 34 years of age when they married 19-year-old brides. Their widowed mothers never remarried despite each surviving their husbands by 24 years. Like Claude, Anna was industrious, capable and determined. Claude liked what he saw in this young saleswoman and courted young Anna whenever her travels brought her to Enid. He finally convinced her to make a trip with him down to Minco to visit his mother, Marguerite. Claude coached Anna with a smattering of French in order that his young sweetheart could impress Marguerite when they were first introduced. Prepared with the French phrase carefully rehearsed with Claude, Anna, upon being introduced to Marguerite, and surrounded by most of Claude's sisters, said in perfect French: "...." or "Kiss my ass." It was a memorable introduction to the Rinn family for Anna, and quite a hit among Claude's sisters. Anna must have forgiven Claude, for a wedding followed on December 31, 1908, with the mother of the groom in attendance.

STARTED FAMILY

Claude and Anna started their family in 1910 with the birth of their first son, Raymond. A daughter named Adean followed in July 1913. Jack Rinn, was born in 1916. During these years, Claude continued his work as one of Enid's leading butchers, working out of the back of his grocery store, changing locations of his store several times to take advantage of the changing demographics of the city. At various times, he had stores on South Quincy, West Broadway and South Buchanan. Despite his success, he extended too much credit to his customers during the depression and found it hard to collect.

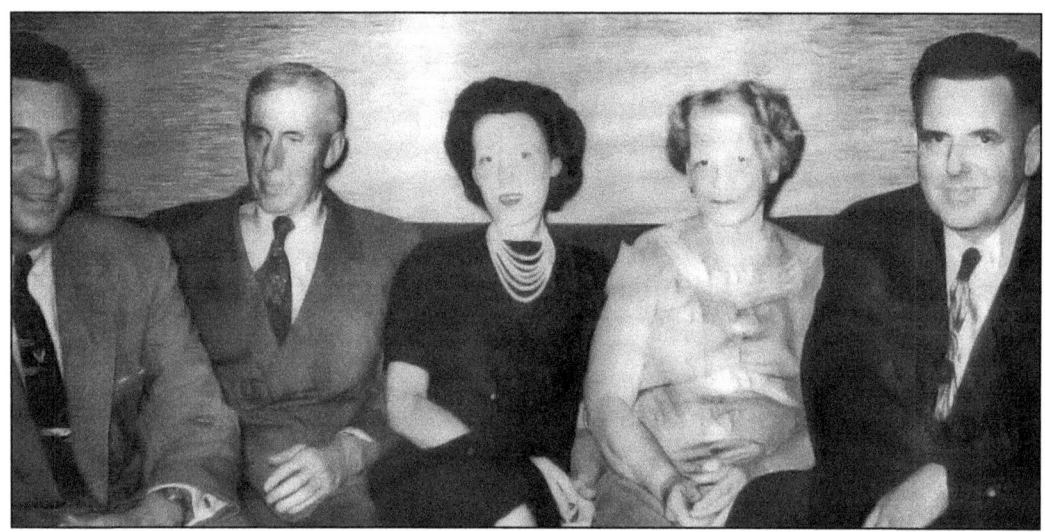

Rinn Family-Jack, Claude, Adean, Anna, Raymond

Stay on Your Side of the Counter

A favorite story of Claude Rinn Told in the Imagined Words of Claude Rinn

"I've just about had enough of Mrs. Gregory. Each week she comes into my meat market here in Enid, Oklahoma, and acts like it is her market, not mine. She tells me what she wants and then steps around the counter to pick out the meat herself. I told her many times, "Mrs. Gregory just stay on your side and I will help you."

Well, I was ready for her the next time. When I saw her coming through the door, I reached down and picked up one of my freshly made link sausages and concealed it inside my apron. She said, "I want four of those chops."

As expected, she then came around the counter just as I lifted my apron and revealed the sausage strategically located in front of my pants. You never saw anyone move so fast as she let out a shriek and fled the store. That may be the end of my troubles with Mrs. Gregory. In fact, I don't expect to see her in my market again."

Went into Cattle Auction Business

He quit the grocery business in 1934 and engaged in the cattle auction business for four years going all over Oklahoma conducting auctions. His niece, Theoda" Chris" (Arthur) Eld, recalled that Claude would come to Chickasha and rely on her to tell him the names of the bidders. Nephew, Don Daggs recalled the story told about Claude's auctions. Claude was always a shrewd businessman. If he didn't get a good bid, he would insert a higher bid in the name of his brother, Edmond Rinn. Edmond did not make the bid or want the cattle, but Claude wanted to drive the bidding up. Sometimes the ploy did not work and Edmond became the owner of the cattle for a short time. A load would be sent to Edmond's farm and then returned later to the auction to get a higher price.

At one time, Claude obtained the concession business at the Enid ballpark where the local baseball team played semi-pro baseball. He was concerned about the well being of his city and began to take an interest in education as his children reached school age. He served on the school board from 1932-1936.

Bought Farm

In 1938 he bought a farm northwest of Lahoma where he engaged in farming and dairy cattle business until his death. He was a member of the First Presbyterian Church, Garfield Lodge No. 501 A.F.& A.M., a 32-degree Mason, and a member of the York Rite, Knight Templar.

Died

Daniel Claude Rinn died on August 20, 1956 at the age of 74. He is buried at Memorial Park Cemetery in Enid, Oklahoma. Anna Rinn died in 1974 and is buried next to her husband.

Children

Raymond Riley Rinn (1910-1963) was born on February 15, 1910 in Enid, Oklahoma, where he grew up. Always a good student, his father helped secure an appointment to West Point for him which he refused. Instead, he earned a degree in Civil Engineering. He married Pauline Lane about 1934 and they had two sons and three daughters.

After residing in Enid, he went to work for the U.S. Bureau of Reclamations working on projects in North Dakota and Colorado and throughout the West. At the age of 57, he suddenly passed away on August 17, 1963. He is buried at Memorial Park Cemetery in Enid, Oklahoma.

Adean (Rinn) Burt (1913-1983) was born April 19, 1913, in Enid, Oklahoma. She worked as an office secretary. At the age of 36, she married Albert Burt on March 18, 1950. She gave birth to a daughter in June 1951 who did not survive. The couple resided in Wichita, Kansas, for a short time before returning to Enid. At the age of 69, she passed away on March 5, 1983 and is buried at Memorial Park Cemetery in Enid.

Raymond Rinn

Adean Rinn

Jack Rinn

Jack Louis Rinn (1916-1992) was born July 20, 1916 in Enid, Oklahoma. He grew up in Enid, and graduated from the University of Oklahoma. He was 6'2" 160 pounds, with blue eyes and dark blonde hair.

On May 15, 1948, he married Gloria Nathalia (Przepiora) Miller and the couple had six children. Living in Wisconsin, Jack had a successful career working for Schlitz Brewing Company becoming vice-president of national accounts and international trade relations.

Jack was an officer in the U.S. Navy during WWII and served in the Atlantic and Pacific as a commander of destroyers escorting military vessels. At the end of the war, he commanded a destroyer that landed on one of the Pacific Turk Islands to disarm the Japanese military. Rinn treated the defeated troops with dignity and compassion. The Japanese army officer, Maj Minoru Kohata, was so touched that he presented Rinn with his most cherished family heirloom, a 300-year-old samurai sword as a token of gratitude. For years, Jack Rinn was unsuccessful in tracking down Kohata so he could correspond with him and return the sword. Finally, in 1988, son Scott Rinn located Kohata in Japan. Jack Rinn and Kohata began corresponding. The samurai sword was returned and Kohata signed his letters "With Love and Respect." In 1992, at a Rinn family reunion in Chickasha, Oklahoma, Rinn and Kohata finally met. Jack Rinn was terminally ill and his son had arranged the surprise visit.

Late in retirement, Jack returned to his hometown of Enid. He passed away at the age of 76 in Enid, Oklahoma, on October 3, 1992. He is buried at the Resurrection Cemetery & Mausoleum, Mequon, Ozaukee County, Wisconsin.

Chapter 16

VIOLET FLORENE RINN
1883-1955

Young Violet

The first of the Rinn children to be born in Kansas, Violet Florene Rinn, arrived on February 25, 1883. A beautiful, tall, blue-eyed, slender girl, Violet grew up in Williamsburg and attended the local schools. Her youngest sister, Jessie Rinn, remembered that Violet was like a second mother to her, always taking care of her when her mother was busy working. Violet adored her father, Lewis Rinn, and rushed to get his pipe and slippers when he came home from work.

Violet was 18 when her family won land in Oklahoma and traveled by covered wagon to their homestead in the fall of 1901. No doubt it was sad for her to leave family and friends. She and her younger sister, Theoda, rode their father's prize race horses for the more than 300-mile trip. For the next few years, she helped her mother and sisters with work on the Rinn farm. Sometimes, she likely ran the household when her parents worked at their meat market in Minco. The Rinn household, with attractive daughters, was well known in the Hazel Dell community where they lived and was the center of social activity. She had fond memories of Williamsburg, Kansas, and her friends there. At times, the Kansas newspaper reported her visits back to Williamsburg.

Married

In 1903, William Sheridan Thompson, accompanied Lewis Rinn to the courthouse in El Reno, and signed as a witness on the Patent Record filed by Rinn to get his homestead. The tall, handsome Thompson was courting Violet. Born in Iowa in 1877, William Sheridan was six years older than Violet and had attended college. At the time of their marriage, he was a farmer living in the nearby community of Leal, Oklahoma Territory. The couple married on January 9, 1906, the same week Lottie and Claire Rinn married. Even though the marriage application was taken out, it was never recorded. This prompted the family to sometimes jokingly say the Thompsons were not legally married.

Son Born

Their son and only child, William Sheridan Thompson, called W.S., was born at Leal, Oklahoma, on October 14, 1907. By 1910, the family was living on a farm in Ninnekah, Grady County, Oklahoma, about 50 miles from the Rinn homeplace at Hazel Dell.

William & Violet Thompson

W.S. Thompson as Baby

Lived in Minco

By the time Marguerite Rinn took sick and needed care, the Thompsons lived in Minco. They nursed her until her death in 1929. In 1930, the census listed them living on 3rd Street (present-day Highway 87) near Caddo Road in Minco. Will was an auto dealer and Violet worked as a bookkeeper for the garage. W.S. lived with them working in construction.

Moved to Colorado

The Thompsons loved Colorado and in the 1930s acquired a parcel of land in the community of Powderhorn in Gunnison County in southwestern Colorado about 230 miles from Denver. They set about creating a resort or dude ranch where guests came to relax, hunt and fish. Square dancing and music took place at night. Will lead pack expeditions into the wilderness while Violet worked cleaning, cooking, and hosting guests. Guests recalled that Violet seemed to continually be working. One guest later remarked when he saw her dressed up that he did not recognize her without a mop or broom in her hands. She was an excellent cook. She was noted for her pies—apple, coconut, and lemon as well as her fried chicken and homemade ice cream.

At times, Rinn family visited Powderhorn. During the cold winter months, the resort closed and the Thompsons relocated to warmer climate and sometimes set out traveling in their trailer. Violet filled her time working on her braided rugs. Will was 76 and Violet 71 when they sold the resort in 1954, but they kept a parcel for their cabin and burial site.

Powderhorn Lodge

Died in 1955

Violet took sick and went to the Anderson Cancer Center in Houston for treatment. When her condition became terminal, Will called her sister, Jessie, for help caring for her. Jessie wanted to care for the older sister that had been like a second mother to her, so she asked Will to bring Violet to Oklahoma. Years later, Jessie recalled the day Will and Violet came by train to Chickasha, Oklahoma. She said Violet was so fragile that Will had to carry her off the train. Jessie nursed her at her home until Violet passed away on November 2, 1955. Violet was buried at the family vault at Powderhorn, Colorado, called Thompson Cemetery.

William Sheridan Thompson continued living in Colorado and died on October 29, 1968 at the age of 91 in Pueblo, Colorado. He is buried alongside Violet at Powderhorn.

Thompson Burial Vault Powderhorn

Son

William Sheridan Thompson Jr., called W.S. (1907-1990), was born October 14, 1907, at Leal, Oklahoma, in Grady County not far from the Rinn homeplace. He grew up in that county and went to the University of Oklahoma to study engineering. He lived with his parents in Minco, Oklahoma in 1930. He was a slender 6'1" with blue eyes and light brown hair. At the age of 26, he married Pauline Magee on July 28, 1934 in Denver Park, Colorado. By October 1940 he was living in Terry, Montana, working as an engineer with the U.S. Bureau of Reclamation, Department of Interior. He and Pauline had two sons. Pauline died in 1952 and W.S. then married Loveta "Delia" Hawkins in Texas. W. S. Thompson died at the age of 82 on October 13, 1990 in Amarillo, Texas. He is buried at Earth Memorial Cemetery at Earth, Lamb County, Texas.

William & Violet Thompson

Chapter 17

THEODA VIRGINIA RINN
1885-1958

Young Theoda

CONTRIBUTED BY JOANN GEDOSH, GRANDDAUGHTER
BEVERLY PEAVLER, GRANDDAUGHTER IN-LAW

Theoda Rinn was born on Sunday, February 22, 1885, in Williamsburg, Kansas. Her parents, Lewis and Marguerite Clair Rinn, named her after Marguerite's younger sister, Theodie. She was the fourth child in the family, which at that point was made up of three girls and one boy.

Theoda grew up in Williamsburg and attended the local schools. According to the local newspaper, Theoda was a good student making the honor roll in 1898. That year, she was in fifth grade in Room III, taught by Miss Hattie Rapp. The class was a combination fifth and sixth grade class with 35 students, including sixth grader, Violet Rinn, who also made the honor roll.

In July 1900, when Theoda was 15, the local newspaper reported that she traveled to Baldwin, Kansas, to visit her Grandmother Clair.

Moved to Oklahoma

Theoda was 16 when her father drew land in the 1901 Oklahoma Land Lottery and moved to a homestead west of Minco, Oklahoma. No doubt, she helped her mother and sisters dry meat and pack supplies for their three-week covered wagon trip to Oklahoma. The younger children rode in the wagons, but Theoda and Violet rode their father's two racehorses.

The Rinns were early settlers in the Hazel Dell community, about 11 miles from Minco. The first few years were primitive as families established their farms, built a school, and started a church. In the winter of 1902, Marguerite and Lewis Rinn ran a meat market in Minco. Some of the time, they needed to stay in town. It was left to Theoda and Violet to care for the younger children and run the household.

Gradually, Theoda's father's health failed, and the family cared for him at home. He had inflammation of the stomach as well as rheumatism. He passed away in February 1905, when Theoda was 20.

Married William Martin

The Hazel Dell farm community created their own social life. Dark-eyed, dark-haired Theoda Rinn was a beautiful young woman with delicate, elegant features. More than likely, she attracted the eye of many of the local young men. But it was through her older sister, the vivacious Violet, that she met her husband-to-be—a tall, dark, and handsome man named William Charles Martin. The Martins, originally from Stokes County, North Carolina, had settled west of Minco in 1902.

According to family legend, Will Martin arrived at the Rinn home one evening to pick up Violet, who had accepted his invitation to attend a local dance. Unfortunately, Will Martin was not Violet's only date that evening. Her "steady" gentleman friend, Will Thompson, had left town for a few days but had come home unexpectedly early. Violet, in a tight spot, talked Theoda into filling in for her. It was Theoda who went to the dance with Will Martin, and that was the beginning of their romance.

In 1904, Will Martin decided to try city life for a while. He moved to Kansas City, Missouri, where he found work driving a horse-drawn streetcar. It seems, though, that Theoda was never far from his thoughts. His frequent letters to her describe his experiences in the big city. On October 6, 1904, he wrote: *"They had a big Ball in the convention hall last night. Fifteen hundred couples can dance at a time there. How would you like to go to a dance like that once? I seen in the paper this morning that there was eight thousand people there last night watching them dance. I am afraid I would lose my partner at a dance like that."*

Will Martin didn't lose his partner. He returned to Oklahoma, and on June 27, 1906, he and Theoda were married. At the time of her marriage, Theoda was the oldest Rinn child left at home, as her sisters Lottie, Claire, and Violet had all married in January 1906 and her brother Claude had left home by then. Will and Theoda traveled to Colorado for their honeymoon and were joined by Frank and Lottie Rinn Pond. They visited Manitou and the Garden of the Gods in Colorado Springs.

LIVED ON RINN FARM

Theoda and Will Martin

The Martins started married life in the Hazel Dell community. A second house was built on the Rinn farm, and the couple lived next to Theoda's mother, Marguerite, while Will farmed the place. A son was born, died, and was buried next to his grandfather, Lewis Rinn, at the Hazel Dell Cemetery one mile up the road. On July 2, 1909, Marguerite Elizabeth was born.

Daughter Marguerite later wrote: "My mother and dad lived on a hill west of Hazel Dell school and cemetery. I was born there…. Uncle Will and Aunt Violet lived one mile north of us. They had a small store. Papa took a bale of cotton to town one day, and Aunt Lottie came to spend the night with Mama, as he would not be back until next day. They asked Aunt Violet to come, but she said she could not. After dark, they heard someone on the back porch and asked, 'Who is there?' No answer, but the door knob began to turn. Aunt Lottie said to Mama (in French), 'Get the gun.' Then they heard a scream, 'It's me, Violet!'"

Honeymoon Trip to Colorado- Will & Theoda Martin, Frank & Lottie Pond

After a few years, Will and Theoda moved to a farm between Ninnekah and Agawam near a railroad. Anna Louise was born there on April 3, 1914. Marguerite recalled: *"I remember having fun watching the trains go by. Our dad would take watermelons up to the railroad tracks and wait for the slow train. The man in back of the train would throw a big piece of ice off, and Dad would run with a watermelon to give him. Many so-called bums came to our house from the railroad track and asked for something to eat. Mama always gave them food, but one time she told the man to cut her some wood while she fixed lunch. When she went out to give food to him, he was about halfway to the railroad track. They later discovered there was a white rag nailed to a pole to let the other bums know you could get food here."*

Life in Hazel Dell

Eventually, the Martins bought their own farm back in the Hazel Dell community, where Will grew corn and picked it with a wagon and a team of horses. He never had a mechanized tractor. Will served on the Hazel Dell School Board, and the family was very active in community affairs. They always hosted a Halloween party for the young people, and many an ice cream social was held at their house.

Will liked baseball, gardening, and playing pool and cards. At butchering time, he delivered meat to many less fortunate members of the community. The Martins were always generous and helpful to those in need.

Theoda, who grew more beautiful with age as her hair turned an attractive gray, was known as an excellent cook, specializing in pastries and breads. She was active in the Hazel Dell Home Demonstration Club after it was organized in April 1923. Often, the Home Demonstration Agent would come and teach new homemaking skills, such as making cheese, canning, and the like. People attending demonstrations met in homes. Since most of the ladies did not drive, their husbands came along and spent the day visiting and doing community improvements such as building terraces or pruning trees.

Theoda always remained close to her sisters. Getting together, they laughed and giggled like young girls. They loved to get on the party telephone line and talk in French, just to annoy neighbors who liked to listen in.

Both Will and Theoda Martin belonged to the Hazel Dell Baptist Church and were faithful and active members. They liked to play the card game Pitch, which was considered a sin by the church at that time. If the preacher made an unexpected visit, they had to scurry to hide the cards.

A somewhat unusual feature of the Martins' life was their penchant for travel. When farm chores were wrapped up for the season, Will, Theoda, and the girls would often drive to Colorado, where

Will had a cousin. He would work in his cousin's feed store in Colorado Springs during the week, and they would explore on the weekends. Louise recalled one eventful trip when Will thought he had left his false teeth in a roadside cabin in New Mexico where they had spent a rainy night. Fortunately, Theoda eventually produced the teeth, which she had picked up on the way out.

The Martins raised Marguerite and Louise to be ladies. They didn't walk the mile to school but rode in a horse-drawn wagon. In the winter, they had a heated iron wrapped in a towel to keep their feet warm. When the snow was deep, Will rode ahead of them to break a trail. They were also well-dressed ladies, thanks in part to Will's younger sister Eva, who was married to Claus Carlson, a department store owner in Minneapolis. Eva would send her old clothes to Theoda, an expert seamstress, who would make them over into beautiful dresses for her daughters.

Later Years

The Martins sold their farm at Hazel Dell and moved to a smaller acreage south of Minco for a few years. Then, in 1949, they retired and moved into a house in Minco. During this time, they went to Buena Vista, Colorado, in the summers. They lived in the in-law cabin on the ranch owned by Louise and her husband. Their 2 grandsons always looked forward to these summer visits.

One grandson remembers that the Martins enjoyed playing canasta and dominos, and most summer evenings the boys spent in their grandparents' cabin playing cards, with the scent of peanuts roasting on the wood stove in the background. Summers were very active, filled with rugged jeep rides on old wagon roads over the high passes. The lunch break always consisted of frying plenty of bacon and potatoes and some kind of meat over an open campfire, with black coffee gurgling in an open coffeepot. Will and Theoda sat on an old wooden wagon seat placed across the two rear fender wells.

But the summers weren't just vacation time. Late summer was fruit season, and the in-law cabin would be sweltering as Louise and Theoda canned fresh peaches, apricots, and plums on the old wood cook stove. Theoda would throw the fruit pits on a rock pile beside the chicken house, and an apricot tree that grew from one of the pits still bares fruit today.

The Martins also sometimes raised turkeys in Colorado during the summers and stayed on to slaughter and sell the turkeys at Thanksgiving and Christmas. One of the grandson's strongest memories of Theoda is from turkey slaughtering time: *"I can still see her pushing bloody turkeys down into a barrel of boiling water and then pulling scalded feathers from turkey after turkey, for half a day. She was absolutely a lady, but she was also a pioneer woman, and she didn't avoid unpleasant jobs. I remember Aunt Violet in the same way."*

In Minco, the Martins had many friends and enjoyed visiting back and forth. Some of these people were old neighbors from the Hazel Dell community. Often, they went to Union City to visit their daughter Marguerite and her family for Sunday dinner. Theoda would bring a delicious homemade cherry or apple pie.

Their granddaughter remembers her grandmother as an amazing woman. She said, *"She had the gentlest spirit, sunny personality, never complaining and always so prim and proper. I remember her telling me in French 'put your dress down.' I can say the phrase today in French but cannot spell it. I guess I was a clumsy, not so proper little girl. She was always my mentor along with my mother. I still grieve her death. A favorite memory was going to Minco on Saturday afternoon with Mother and Grandmother. The ritual was for them to get their hair fixed. Then we would go to the grocery store for a cherry Coke. They always argued over who would pay the fifteen cents. Granddad would be playing pool and just maybe might have a beer."*

Will and Theoda celebrated their fiftieth wedding anniversary in June 1956. Photos from later years reveal a still-handsome couple with strength and humor shining from their faces.

Will had a hard time retiring from farming. He was often depressed at not being able to work and earn money. Theoda developed several medical problems. She had had a kidney removed earlier in her life. Later, due to a car accident, her spleen had to be removed. She developed leukemia. When she was asked how she felt, though, she always said, *"Honey, I think I feel better today."* She died at her home in Minco on August 2, 1958, at the age of 73. She is buried at the Evergreen Cemetery in Minco.

After Theoda's death, Will continued living in their home in Minco. He raised wheat in the back yard and made his own cereal and flour. Will was admitted to Parkview Hospital in El Reno and passed away on October 23, 1962. He was 84 at the time. He is buried in the Evergreen Cemetery in Minco beside his wife.

Theoda and Will in Later Years

Daughters

Marguerite Martin (1909-1999) was born July 2, 1909 on the Rinn farm at Hazel Dell, Grady County, Oklahoma. She grew up attending the Hazel Dell School, and Minco High School. She lived with her uncle, Edmond Rinn, when she earned a teaching credential from Oklahoma College for Women at Chickasha, Oklahoma. Prior to marriage, she taught school. On December 24, 1933, Marguerite married Thomas Arthur Pinkston, at Cogar, Oklahoma. Witnesses were her cousin Gene Pond and Hazel Chappell. Because Marguerite might lose her teaching job if it was known she was married, the marriage was kept secret for a short time. Eventually, the couple farmed north of Minco near Union City. Three children would come from this marriage. After raising her family, Marguerite returned to teaching. Marguerite passed away at the age of 89 on April 28, 1999. She is buried at the Evergreen Cemetery in Minco, Oklahoma.

Marguerite 10, Louise 5

Anna Louise Martin (1914-2005) was born April 3, 1914, in Grady County, Oklahoma. Louise earned her teaching credential. On March 24, 1938, at the age of 23, Louise married William Marion Peavler also from Grady County. They had two sons. In 1947, the Peavlers moved to Buena Vista, Colorado, where both taught in the public schools. Louise passed away on October 28, 2005 at the age of 91 in Colorado. She is buried at the Evergreen Cemetery in Minco, Oklahoma.

Chapter 18

Lewis David Rinn

1887-1973

Young Lewis

The second son and sixth child of Lewis and Marguerite Rinn, Lewis David Rinn, was born on December 26, 1887, in Williamsburg, Kansas. Called Toby by the family, he attended Williamsburg schools and completed 8th grade. It must have been hard to leave his friends at age 14 when his family moved to Oklahoma. Likely he worked hard helping his family establish their homestead in Oklahoma Territory. His father died when he was 18. By 1910 he was 22 and living away from home working as a farm laborer on the Gordon farm at Lone Rock in Caddo County, Oklahoma. Lewis was medium build with dark thick hair and dark eyes and the "Rinn hooked nose."

STOLE CATTLE

Maybe Lewis needed the money or liked the adventure when he and a group of other young men rustled cattle from a nearby farm in February 1912. They stole the cattle and drove them to Hinton, Oklahoma, and sold them for $140. Within the week, they were caught and brought to trial. *The Minco Minstrel* Newspaper carried the story on February 12, so everyone knew about the crime. Lewis's younger brother, Edmond, was also involved. Both plead guilty. Family lore says Lewis took most of the blame for the crime in order to save his brother. Edmond was placed on probation and Lewis sent to Granite Reformatory. Throughout his life, Edmond remembered the favor, and helped Lewis when he could.

MARRIAGE & MILITARY SERVICE

Lewis married Leoda Sanders of Billings, Oklahoma, on May 31, 1918 in Chickasha, Oklahoma. Present at the ceremony were his mother, Marguerite Rinn, and his sisters, Violet, and Theoda. He enlisted in the military the next day and departed for Camp Shelby, Louisiana, for training. Leoda, accompanied by Jessie Rinn and Susie Dobbins, returned to Billings before joining her husband in Louisiana. Daughter, Marvel Rinn was born on November 30, 1918 while the couple were stationed in Texas. After serving in Louisiana and Texas, Lewis was released from the army on February 11, 1919.

LIVED IN BILLINGS, OKLAHOMA

Lewis as Young Man

Leoda grew up in Billings, so the couple moved there after WWI. Their family grew with the birth of Claire on January 13, 1920, and Lewis David Jr. on December 23, 1920—three children under the age of four. The family continued living in Billings during the 1920s and early 1930s. Then they relocated to Grady County, Oklahoma, where they lived on the Rinn farm which belonged to Edmond Rinn, for a short time.

LIVED IN GRADY COUNTY, OKLAHOMA

By 1935, Lewis moved to a farm in Ninnekah across the road from where Lewis's sister, Seona's family lived. When Lewis signed up in 1942 for the WWII Draft enrollment, he was a farmer living in Ninnekah. Only Leoda and son, L.D. lived with him by that time.

Lived in Long Beach, California

After WWII, it seemed everyone moved to California where the economy was booming. Lewis and Leoda Rinn were part of the migration to Southern California. Marvel and husband, and L.D. and Claire followed. The Rinns lived on Cameron Street, on a small acreage in the north part of Long Beach. Lewis worked as a maintenance man and laughed as he told people he painted outhouses for a construction company. He raised banty roosters, but his real joy was gambling at the nearby card casino. From time to time, his Rinn family visited from Oklahoma.

Rinns in Long Beach-Lewis, Leoda, Marvel, L.D.

1953 Visit to California-Seona, Lewis, Edmond, Jessie

Family Loss

Son, L.D., died in September 1954. Wife, Leoda passed away in 1956. Lewis lived to be 86 years old and passed away on March 5, 1973, in Long Beach. He is buried Westminster Memorial Park, Westminster, California.

Children

Marvel Rinn (1918-1978) was born November 30, 1918 in Texas but grew-up in Billings, Oklahoma. She completed two years of college. In1940, she lived in Billings residing in a rooming house working as dental assistant. She married James Whitlow. They had a daughter, and son and resided in Long Beach, California. She died July 7, 1978, in Los Angeles, and is buried Park at Westminster, Westminster, CA..

Claire Ivah Rinn (1920-1996) was born January 13, 1920 in Billings, Oklahoma. In 1940, she was a student nurse taking training in Enid, Oklahoma. This led to a life-long nursing career. She had no children. She married in 1980, moved to Sarasota, Florida, and passed away at the age of 76 on July 27, 1996, in Sarasota, Florida.

Lewis David "L. D." Rinn Jr. (1920-1954) was born December 23. 1920, in Oklahoma. He grew up in Billings, and Ninnekah, Oklahoma, where he completed high school. He was 5'6" and slight build. He enlisted in the Air Corp on December 15, 1941, as a private and served until September 15, 1945. Living in Long Beach, he continued in the reserves in the Air Force as a Technical Sargent. He had no children. He died October 19, 1953, at age of 32 in San Francisco. He is buried at Westminster Park, Westminster, CA.

Young Rinn Children- L.D., Marvel, Claire

Chapter 19

EDMOND VALTON RINN
1891-1967

Young Edmond

BORN IN KANSAS

Edmond Valton Rinn was born on Wednesday, July 29, 1891, at the home of his parents, Lewis and Marguerite Rinn, in Williamsburg, Kansas. Older sisters, Lottie 14 and Claire 12, probably helped care for him.

Edmond attended the local Williamsburg Schools. According to the *Williamsburg Star* newspaper, he was neither absent nor tardy for the month of April 1899. His teacher was Florence Fitzgerald and there were more than 60 students in Room I.

GREW UP IN OKLAHOMA

Edmond was 10 years old when his family relocated to their homestead about 11 miles northwest of Minco, Oklahoma, in November, 1901. He slept in an outside shelter the first months while his mother and sisters slept in covered wagons before their sod and log cabin was finished. For the first two years, there was no school for him to attend. No doubt he enjoyed the freedom of running and playing near their creek-side homestead. His father was part of a group of parents who signed a note to construct a school. It was called Hazel Dell and opened in the fall of 1903 with 30 students attending for six months. Edmond walked one mile north to the one room schoolhouse that was heated by a potbellied woodburning stove in the center of the room with kerosene lights illuminating the room during the dark days of winter. He probably went on to complete three years of high school.

His father, Lewis Rinn, died in the winter of 1905 when Edmond was 13. He continued living with his widowed mother and brother and two sisters at the Rinn farm. Although he helped with the farming, he never liked it.

Got in Trouble

Maybe Edmond liked the adventure or simply went along with his older brother, Lewis, when a group of young men rustled cattle from a nearby farm in February 1912. They stole the cattle and drove them to Hinton, Oklahoma, and sold them for $140. Within the week, they were caught and brought to trial. *The Minco Minstrel* Newspaper carried the story on February 12. Edmond's older brother, Lewis, was involved. Both pleaded guilty. Family lore says Lewis took most of the blame for the crime in order to protect Edmond. Edmond was placed on probation and Lewis sent to Granite Reformatory. Throughout his life, Edmond remembered the favor, and helped Lewis when needed.

Served in World War I

When WWI broke out in Europe and the United States entered the war, Edmond registered for the draft on June 5, 1917. He said he was a single 25-year-old farmer. He described himself as normal build with blue eyes and red hair. [on the WWII Draft Registration form, he said he was 5'11", weighed 174, had brown eyes, and red hair]. He entered the Army and was sent to France and then to occupied Germany.

Edmond Rinn and his company saw fierce combat in France. They were in the thickest battles and sustained injuries and casualties. Many of Edmund's buddies were killed. At one point, Edmond felt the stress of battle and tried to flee his fox hole. His best friend, Burt Thompson, may have saved his life. Burt threw himself on top of Edmond, preventing him from sure death from the raging gun fire overhead. The two remained lifelong friends.

WWI Fought in France, Stationed in Occupied Germany-Edmond center

MARRIED SUSIE DOBBINS

With the war over in 1919, Edmond returned home to his anxious family. He courted Susan Dobbins who lived with her family on a neighboring farm in the Hazel Dell community. Susie, a pretty faired haired girl, was born in Missouri in 1900. When Edmond was 29 and Susie was 21, the couple married on April 21, 1921. They moved to Chickasha, Oklahoma. Edmond Valdon Jr., called E.V., was born November 8, 1921, and Eugene Claude was born July 13, 1925. Eugene was called Gene and was named after his 15-year-old cousin, Eugene Pond, and his uncle, Claude Rinn.

PROBATED MOTHER'S ESTATE

Edmond was almost 38 when his mother, Marguerite, died on May 16, 1929. Three weeks later, Edmond went to the courthouse in Chickasha and appeared before Judge Chastain, petitioning to be appointed administrator of her estate in the absence of a will. On June 3rd, 1929, he was appointed administrator. By November 27th, 1929, Edmond finished filing the more than 30 pages of legal documents and completed the probate and distributed the estate to the heirs. Each brother or sister received a one-ninth share of the Rinn farm. Edmond bought out each heir and owned the farm for many years.

LIVED IN CHICKASHA

By 1930, the family lived at 1017 Fourth Street where they owned their Chickasha home worth about $2000. They also owned a radio. Edmond was working as an auto salesman and E.V. was attending school. It was also noted that Edmond was a veteran of WWI. Later, the family moved to their home at 1427 S. 18th Street.

OWNED AUTO DEALERSHIP

Edmond was very successful as an auto salesman working first for the Oldsmobile dealer in Chickasha and selling used cars on the side. Eventually, he owned the dealership. He was a born salesman. People came from all over the area to buy a car from him because they believed he would give them the best deal. Although he was not a great talker, everyone knew and liked him.

Edmond Rinn Successful Businessman

Successful in business, Edmond helped his family. Numerous nieces stayed with Edmond and Susie while they went to college in Chickasha at Oklahoma College for Women. Some worked for him. Otherwise, they would not have been able to complete their schooling. He loaned money to others when they were in need. In 1934, when nephew, Gene Pond, married and moved to a farm east of Chickasha, Edmond gathered up furnishings and made sure his nephew had what was needed. During the 1950s, Edmond provided a home for his sister, Seona. when she didn't have a place to live.

Susie is remembered as the kind hearted, loving person in the family. Every summer she spent many a hot day helping her sister-in-law, Seona, can fruits, vegetables, and meat so the family would have food. During the war, she drove the Daggs family to Louisiana so they could visit Vera Mae and her husband there.

BOUGHT POOL HALL

World War II halted the production of automobiles and Edmond was a shrewd enough businessman to anticipate that his auto business would decline. He bought a pool hall in town and successfully ran it. After the war, Edmond returned to the auto business and owned several farms as well.

Rinn Family Gatherings at Edmond's Home

Many Rinn family gatherings took place at the Rinn home in Chickasha. In 1953, Edmond and Susie drove Jessie and Seona to California so they could visit their brother, Lewis, in Long Beach.

DIED IN 1967

At the age of 75, Edmond died on February 18, 1967. He is buried at the Fairlawn Cemetery in Chickasha, Oklahoma. Susie continued living in Chickasha enjoying life. She was always a favorite in the Rinn family. Living to be 90 years old, she died on November 10, 1990, and is buried beside Edmond.

Sons

Edmond Valdon "E. V." Rinn Jr. (1921-1970) was born November 8, 1921 and called E.V. He grew up in Chickasha and married Joy Mex Bullock in 1941. The young couple lived in San Francisco during WWII but returned to Chickasha in 1945 to establish their home. They had two sons. E.V. died of cancer at the age of 48 on February 12, 1970. Joy continued living in Chickasha earning a degree in teaching from Oklahoma College for Women. She taught school in Ninnekah for 17 years and was on the Chickasha City Council for four years. Joy died in 2002 and is buried in the Rosehill Cemetery in Chickasha beside E. V.

Eugene Claude "Gene" Rinn

Edmond Valeton Jr.,"E.V." Rinn

Eugene Claude "Gene" Rinn (1925-2006) was born July 13, 1925 in Chickasha. Gene married Wanda Hickman in 1949. They lived in Chickasha where their two daughters, grew up. Gene developed lung cancer and passed away on December 15, 2006 and is buried in Rosehill Cemetery, Chickasha.

Chapter 20

SEONA HELEN RINN

1893-1984

Young Seona

The fifth daughter and ninth child of Lewis and Marguerite Rinn, Seona Helen Rinn, was born on Sunday, September 10, 1893 in Williamsburg, Kansas. She began her education at the Williamsburg School located around the corner from the Rinn home on Main Street. She had just turned eight and began third grade when her family sold their meat market, packed their belongings, and traveled to their homestead in Oklahoma Territory during the fall of 1901. In later years, she recalled that the girls slept in the covered wagons during the three-week journey.

Grew Up in Oklahoma

Likely, the first Christmas in Oklahoma, Seona and her sister Jessie, received dolls from Santa. The dolls, which may have been expensive German dolls, stand about two feet high and have ceramic faces and hands with delicate complexions. Blond curls frame the faces. The original garments have been replaced. Seona made the blue-checked gingham dress and hat now worn by her doll. The doll is missing a big toe as a result of her sister, Jessie, biting it off when the girls got into a fight. Both sisters, living to be over ninety, kept their cherished dolls and passed them on to their families. These antiques are now almost 120 years old. Seona's doll is displayed in her son's home in Oklahoma. The doll sits on a child's chair that was once part of the Rinn's ice cream store in Williamsburg, Kansas.

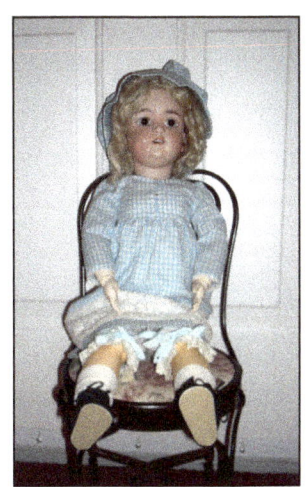

Seona's Doll

Seona (left) & Jessie

In Oklahoma Territory, for the first two years, Seona had no school to attend. It is not known whether the Rinn children received any home schooling during this time because there was so much work to be done establishing a home and farm. In the fall of 1903, a one room school, Hazel Dell, was opened one mile north of the Rinn homestead. By 1906-7 there were 61 students enrolled. Seona completed her schooling there in the eighth grade.

Seona was 11 when her father, Lewis Rinn, passed away from stomach cancer. Her mother, Marguerite Rinn aged 48, applied for and got a Civil War pension for her minor children including Seona. After 1906, only Lewis Jr., Edmond, Seona and Jessie lived at home with their mother. By 1910, Lewis Jr., hired out on a farm in the nearby Lone Rock township. Sometime before 1910, Seona completed her schooling at the Hazel Dell School.

The dark eyed, dark haired Seona had a prominent Aquiline nose typical of some of her siblings, especially brother Lewis Jr. Always energetic and hardworking, she helped her mother and worked on the family farm. Despite moving from Kansas at an early age, she kept in touch with her older cousin, Jennie Gonon in Ottawa, Kansas. In Seona's belongings, there was a 1911 postcard addressed to her from her cousin and it referred to a visit by Seona to Kansas that year.

Married and Moved to Iowa

In 1914, at the age of 21, Seona married 21-year-old Ruel Daggs. They moved to Galva, Iowa, to work on a farm. On the 1915 Iowa State Census, Ruel states that he made an income of $400 the previous year. Seona was far from her family and missed them, but they stayed in touch and some summers Lewis Jr., and Jessie came up to help with the harvest. It was said that Seona could keep up with any man shucking corn or other farm work. Their first child, Vera Mae Daggs, was born on November 2, 1916. No doubt trips were made back to Oklahoma. In 1924, Marguerite Rinn wrote to Seona expressing hope that the Daggs could visit her in Oklahoma. It is not known whether they made the visit.

Seona and Ruel Daggs about 1914

MOVED BACK TO OKLAHOMA

By 1927 the Daggs moved back to Oklahoma near Minco. Donald Daggs was born December 9, 1927. Eleven-year-old Vera Mae was used to being an only child and was not sure she liked having a baby brother who was getting attention. Sometimes Louise Martin, Seona's niece, stayed with Vera Mae. Louise enjoyed playing with Don so Vera Mae began to think Don was okay. Don remembered his Dad taking him everywhere he went riding on his horse. He also had a vague memory of his Dad holding him when they viewed Marguerite Rinn's coffin at her funeral May 16, 1929.

In April 1930, the Daggs family lived in El Reno while Ruel worked on the state highway. By the time Rueleen Daggs was born on October 21, 1930, the family lived on a farm about five miles west and one mile north of Minco.

TOOK IN NEPHEW

Times were tough and Seona always had a lot of work to do, but in 1933, she took in her nephew, Gene Pond, the son of her deceased older sister Lottie Rinn Pond. He had returned from California and needed a place to stay. Don Daggs remembered his Dad and Gene having a money-making scheme to raise baby turkeys to be sold for Thanksgiving. On horseback, Gene herded the turkeys from one fallow field to another. When Thanksgiving arrived, few people had the money to purchase a turkey to eat. The two men devised a scheme to make a profit and get rid of the birds at the same time. On successive weekends, they held a turkey shoot. Targets were set up in the field across from the Daggs' house. People would drive out to the farm, pay to take their chances on target shooting and those that won took home a turkey. Seona sold drinks and homemade desserts.

Red-headed Rueleen remembers Gene Pond living with them and how he would carry her around on his shoulders and spoil her. When he left to marry Hazel Chappell in October 1934, Rueleen cried because she didn't want him to leave.

LIVED NEAR NINNEKAH

David Daggs was born in April 1934 and James Daggs was born 18 months later in 1936. In 1938, the family moved to a farm near Ninnekah. Seona was a hard worker with five children, the farm work, and cooking to do. Her family remembers her as a wonderful cook. In the summer she and Susie Rinn, Edmond's wife, would spend long, hot days canning to lay in a supply of food for the winter. Don especially liked her canned meat. Coming home on the school bus, her children would be greeted everyday by some of Seona's baked goods. A favorite was her sugar pie made from left over dough and sugar.

Seona wanted her children to do well. She let them know if they worked hard they would succeed. The family did not attend church, but they were taught to treat everyone fair. Despite Ruel's habit of swearing, the children were not allowed to swear.

In the mid 1940s, Seona developed breast cancer. She was hospitalized for surgery. Later she took the bus from Chickasha to Oklahoma to get radiation treatment. She received numerous well wishes from friends and neighbors and many from those she grew up with in the Hazel Dell community. At the time of her death more than 50 years later, she still had these get-well cards in her possession.

Close to Family

Seona was always close to her family, but that did not mean she didn't get mad at them. At times, she would have nothing to do with her brother Lewis or sister Jessie. They would go for long periods of time without speaking. Nobody would apologize, but eventually they would be friendly again. Her children have fond memories of going to Chickasha on Saturdays and stopping off to see Aunt Jessie at work and then go down the street to Uncle Edmond's pool hall. Other times the family went to Jessie and Bruce Arthur's for the grown ups to play the card game of Pitch. Jim Daggs remembers that as soon as their car turned up the driveway, he heard laughter radiating from the house.

Seona about 60 years old

In 1953, Edmond and Susie Rinn brought Seona and Jessie with them to California to visit their brother Lewis Rinn in Long Beach. They had a grand time greeting family in the French manner of kissing everyone. There was a family reunion held in a park in Anaheim reuniting them with their nephews, Gene and Don Pond, as well as Lewis's children and families and Susie's sister Annabel Eisenhour and family.

Worked at University

When Jim graduated from high school, Ruel Daggs sold off the farm equipment and decided to separate from the family. Edmond and Susie Rinn offered Seona and Jim a place to stay while Jim started college. In 1957, Jim entered the University of Oklahoma at Norman so he and Seona moved there. Seona got a job working at the University food service and continued there until she retired. Always ambitious, she got side jobs cleaning houses. Her grandnephew, Bill Thompson, was also at the University and she invited him over for home cooked meals and helped him do his laundry on weekends. She did not start to turn grey until well into her 60s.

She never drove a car but walked everywhere including the grocery store. In fact, her daughter-in-law remembers having a hard time keeping up with her. She had an infectious laugh that was distinctive. On one occasion, her grandnephew was visiting the University of Oklahoma from Colorado. As he went down the cafeteria line, he recognized Seona's laugh and soon saw Aunt Seona working behind the line.

After Seona retired, she continued living in Norman in her house. Her daughter, Vera Mae, bought a house there and planned to retire near her mother, but Alzheimer disease struck and Vera Mae passed away in 1980.

LOVING MEMORIES

A granddaughter's remembrance:

Oh, I have such wonderful memories of my granny! Her cooking and those sugar pies. And her knitting, she always had a knitting project going. She didn't drive so she would ride the bus to come visit us. I remember one time she was visiting and I had brought home my report card that day. In one subject I had received a poor grade and during supper, my dad told me that after the meal was over, I would receive a spanking. Well that did not sit well with my granny. She told him if he spanked me, she was going to catch the next bus home. And when she got home, she would mail me all his report cards with bad grades from his school years. I didn't get spanked, she saved me! She was a very loving granny to my sister and I.

When Seona lived in Norman and her children came to visit and offered to take her for a ride, she often asked to go out to Hazel Dell. She loved the place where she grew up.

Always strong and independent, Seona was not happy when it was necessary to move to a convalescent home in Spiro, Oklahoma. Her granddaughter owned the facility and saw that Seona had the best care. When Don Daggs visited, Seona wanted him to feed her although he knew she really didn't need help. He told her, "*If this place was the Waldorf Astoria, you still wouldn't like it.*" At the age of 90 ½, Seona passed away on March 21, 1984, and is buried at the Evergreen Cemetery, Minco, Oklahoma.

Children

Vera Mae Daggs (1916-1972) was born November 2, 1916 in Ida County, Iowa. Her early years were spent in Iowa until the family moved back to Oklahoma. She was an only child her first 11 years. She taught school before marrying Bernice Eubanks in 1939. The couple had two sons. Her husband died in 1946, leaving Vera Mae with a family to raise. She returned to teaching. Eventually, she bought a house in Norman, Oklahoma, and planned to retire near her mother. But Vera Mae developed Alzheimer disease and passed away at the age of 63 on May 10, 1980. She is buried at Evergreen Cemetery, Minco, Oklahoma.

Donald Alan Daggs (1927-2006) was born December 9, 1927 in Minco, Oklahoma. He grew up near Ninnekah, Oklahoma. He registered for the draft in December 1945 and served in the military. He married Edalane Aust and they had one son. Don worked 20 years for Superior Oil Company before establishing his own company, Daggs Production Services, Inc. of Fort Smith, Arkansas, in 1976. He passed away at the age of 79 on May 29, 2006, in Fort Smith, Arkansas.

Vera Mae Daggs

Don Daggs

Ruleen Daggs (1930) was born October 21, 1930 in Minco, Oklahoma. She grew up near Ninnekah, Oklahoma and graduated from Oklahoma College for Women. She taught school before marrying fellow teacher, Lee James Freeze. They had one son and adopted twin sons. Living in Big Spring, Texas, she continued teaching school until retirement.

David Daggs (1934) was born April 28, 1934 in Minco, Oklahoma and grew up near Ninnekah, Oklahoma. He married Betty Linton in 1956 and they had two daughters. After a successful career in the oil business in Oklahoma and Arkansas, he retired to live in Edmond, Oklahoma.

James Keith Daggs (1936) was born Feb 3, 1936 and grew up near Ninnekah, Oklahoma. He graduated from the University of Oklahoma in 1959 and became a Certified Public Accountant owning his own firm Daggs Associates in Aspen, Colorado. He married Gae Wilson on September 17, 1966 in Midland, Texas. The couple had no children. He resides in Colorado.

Rueleen Daggs

Jim Daggs

David Daggs

Chapter 21

JESSIE MAE RINN

1896-1992

Young Jessie

Jessie Mae Rinn was born on January 1, 1896 in Williamsburg, Kansas. She was the youngest of ten children. Her father, Lewis Rinn, was 55, and her mother, Marguerite (Clair) Rinn, was 40. Her 13-year-old sister, Violet, seemed like a mother to Jessie because she often took care of her when her mother worked in the ice cream store.

MOVED TO OKLAHOMA

Jessie was just five when the family left Kansas in 1901 and traveled by covered wagon to their homestead west of Minco, Oklahoma. The first Christmas she found out about Santa Claus when she received a doll. She liked to tell this story.

How I Found Out About Santa
Told in the Imagined Words of Jessie Rinn

It is Christmas 1901 and we just moved to Oklahoma Territory from Kansas. I am five and the red-headed baby of our family. I told Mama that I really want a doll from Santa, but I am not sure Santa knows where we live. We are on our new land out in the country and we don't even have a real house yet. Papa and the hired help are working to make a house for us, but we still have to sleep outside—we girls in the covered wagons and the boys bundle up outside.

It's really fun here. There's no school so my big sister, Seona who's eight, and I can play all day. We like to play in the red dirt and run back and forth from the creek. Papa says there will be a school built just up the road by the time I am old enough to go.

Last time Papa went to the post office at Leal he brought home a Christmas package for all of us. It came from Lottie and Claire in Kansas. My two oldest sisters didn't come with us to Oklahoma. They're working there until Papa finishes building our house.

Jessie's Doll

They sent all of us wonderful gifts. You should see my beautiful doll that Mama says is from Santa. Now, I'm trying to figure out Santa. Does he live in Kansas and does he know Lottie and Claire? I've been thinking about it, and I suppose I have figured out Santa, but I'm not going to tell.

Jessie about 5

Jessie's sister, Seona, owned a similar doll. The dolls, which may have been expensive German dolls, stand about two feet high and have ceramic faces and hands with delicate complexions. Blond curls frame the faces. Jessie's doll, which was partially restored at some time, has long ash blond hair. How could the family afford such expensive dolls when they were struggling to establish their homestead in 1901?

We'll never know, but older Rinn children, Lottie, and Claire, had jobs and were making money in Kansas when they sent gifts that first Christmas. Probably they splurged on the dolls for their youngest sisters.

Father Died

Jessie was nine when her father died. The family continued residing on their farm. Her four older sisters and brother married leaving the four younger children living with their widowed mother. She grew up in the Hazel Dell Community having lots of friends. The H.S. McDaniel family lived to the west of the Rinns and Jessie said they all loved one another just like brothers and sisters. When she completed schooling, she wanted to teach at a country school and had a teaching job lined up. It seemed her mother thought she should stay at home so she faked an illness until it was too late for Jessie to start teaching. Many years later Jessie said, "Mother was spoiled by my Dad. She was much younger than him, and he worshipped the ground she walked on."

In 1921 when Jessie was 25, she was baptized at the Hazel Dell Baptist Church. She taught the teenagers Sunday school class and liked to treat them to homemade ice cream.

Married

On November 26, 1922, Jessie married Thomas Bruce Arthur. The red-headed Jessie was 26 and Bruce was 29. They were married at the Rinn homeplace by J.W. Barker, minister of the Hazel Dell Church. Edmond Rinn and Theoda Rinn Martin were witnesses. They lived on the Rinn homestead several years where Theoda "Chris" was born July 15, 1923 and Jesse Ruel was born January 30, 1925. Jesse Ruel was named after Dr. Jesse Little who was the Minco doctor who delivered the babies at home.

Jessie (left) & Seona

Jessie about 19

Jessie & Bruce Arthur

Moved Near Chickasha

About 1930 the Arthurs moved to the Friend Community near Chickasha, Oklahoma, where they resided 13 years. Then they purchased a farm north of Chickasha across from the airport where many family gatherings took place. A nephew recalled going to Jessie and Bruce's with his parents on Friday nights for them to play cards. He said, "As soon as we drove up the hill to their farm, I could hear the laughter." Sometimes, Bruce, called square dances.

Jessie was a homemaker, mother, and helped with the farm chores. As the children grew up, Jessie, who was always full of energy, convinced Bruce she needed to go to work or loss her mind. She said, "I'll even buy the groceries if you'll let me work." She worked at Clayton's Dry Goods Store, Penny's and 13 years with Modern Appliance Store. She was a member of the First Baptist Church.

Bruce Arthur died at the age of 64 on October 6, 1957. He is buried at Fairlawn Cemetery in Chickasha. Six years later Jessie married A.J. Spurlin. They set out traveling to every state, to Canada, and spending seven winters in Mexico. A. J. passed away in 1987.

Widowed twice, Jessie continued being active and enjoying life. She once said, "I am so glad that I now have gray hair instead of red because I can wear pink. She passed away on October 30, 1992 at the age of 96 and is buried at Fairlawn Cemetery, Chickasha, Oklahoma. Her grandniece, JoAnn Pinkston Gedosh wrote a tribute to Jessie.

A Tribute to a Grand Lady

JoAnn (Pinkston) Gedosh, 1992

She has been called Grandmother, Aunt Jessie, the Best of Cooks, the Flower Lady, Queen of the Rinn Reunion, and for sure, she reigned as the Last of the Rinn Matriarchs. As much as she traveled, she certainly also could have been called a "Goin" Jessie". She has been the inspiration for the Rinn Reunions for the past several years. We came together for more of her stories and never tired of the ones of her and her giggling French speaking sisters and how her father, Grandpa Rinn, won land in the Oklahoma Lottery and brought Grandma Rinn by covered wagon with nine children from Kansas to Hazel Dell, Oklahoma.

One of her great-great nieces, as a small child, recalled Aunt Jessie as her favorite aunt because she taught her to needlepoint in an hour. Her handiwork is visible from her flower garden, her paintings, and needlepoint to the salmon A.J. caught and she canned. If stray dogs and cats could talk, they could also tell some good stories about what a good buddy she has been to them through the years.

Jessie as Active 94-year-old

We will all miss her Christmas card this year. It always arrived shortly after Thanksgiving. At the age of 96, she said to one of her nieces upon the niece's comment about her early, predictable card, "Hon, you know, I always bought them after Christmas, but I just didn't do it this year." She knew she had lived a long, full life and was ready to journey on to her next life. As the Grand Lady passes the torch to the next generation, we feel deeply challenged to keep the family connected. Aunt Jessie, you'll be with us at every Rinn reunion and we'll tell the same stories, not as well, but we'll add new ones, and we'll thank you for the gift of your life and the commitment to this family. You were so loved!

Children

Theoda Florence "Chris" Arthur (1923-2003) was born July 15, 1923 on the Rinn homeplace near Minco, Oklahoma. Her first year of school, she attended Hazel Dell School where her mother and other Rinns went. When she was about seven, her family moved to Chickasha where she grew up. Named after her aunt, Theoda Rinn, she adopted the name Chris as a young person.

She married Charles Eld, a career Air Force officer, in 1947. They had two sons. After moving with the military, the couple settled in Colorado Springs, Colorado, in 1964. Chuck passed away in 1989. Chris continued living in Colorado Springs and attended many Rinn family reunions. She passed away at the age of 79 on January 3, 2003 and is buried at the Fairlawn Cemetery, Chickasha, Oklahoma.

Jesse Ruel Arthur (1925-1987) was born January 30, 1925 on the Rinn homeplace. He grew up in Chickasha and married Frances Miser on October 3, 1949. He farmed in Pauls Valley, Oklahoma. The couple had a daughter and two sons. At the age of 52, Jesse Ruel passed away on September 18, 1977 and is buried at Whitebead Cemetery, Pauls Valley, Oklahoma.

Theoda "Chris" Arthur

Jesse Ruel Arthur

Part V

Not Forgotten—Rinn Family Gatherings

"We feel deeply challenged to keep the family connected."

~JoAnn Gedosh, great-granddaughter

The Rinn Children

Marguerite & Lewis Rinn's Children 1940s
L-R: Violet, Lewis, Jessie, Seona, Edmond, Claire, Claude, Theoda. Missing is Lottie who died in 1920

Together in California in 1953
L-R: Seona, Lewis, Edmond, Jessie

Rinn Descendants

1998 Rinn Descendants-Estes Park Colorado
Identified by Ancestor
Front: Anna & Dan Rinn
Seated LR: John Rinn, Bing & Rae Ann Larson, Bill & Linda Pinkston, Nick & Janelle Richardson, JoAnn & Jack Gedosh
Standing LR: Dan & Beth Rinn, Scott Rinn, Janette and Skip Lusk, Virginia & Bill Thompson, Dian Gofhus, Winnie Haire, Gae & Jim Daggs, Chris Eld, Lisa Arthur

*Some of the 36 Descendants Attending Rinn Reunion, Lake Tenkiller, Oklahoma, in 1996
FR: Hazel Pond, Glenda & Jackie Emory, Marguerite Pinkston,
2nd Row LR: Linda Pinkston, Lisa Arthur, Frances Grimes, Rueleen Freeze, Paula Phillips, Rae Ann Larson,
Janelle Richardson, unidentified, Betty Daggs, Norma June Jones,
BR: Richard Grimes, Jay Freeze, Don Daggs, unidentied, Scott Rinn, David Daggs, Dan Rinn*

Some of Marguerite & Lewis Rinn's Great Grandchildren 1995
LR: Judy Steuber, Jim Peavler, Terry Peavler, Rae Ann Larson, John Rinn, Lisa Arthur, Paula Phillips, JoAnn Gedosh, Winnie Haire

Heuchelheim, Germany, 2000
3 generations of Rinns Returned to Germany & France

Endnotes

1 Ford County, Kansas, Marriage Certificate (1876), Rinn-Clair; Ford County Probate Judge, Dodge City.

2 Jessie (Rinn) Spurlin, daughter of Lewis and Marguerite Rinn (Chichasha, Oklahoma), interview by unknown interviewer, prior to 1991; audio privately held by Janelle Richardson, Morro Bay, California. 2012.

3 Joseph Vernon, *Dodge City and Ford County Kansas: A History of the Old and a Story of the New* (Larned: Tucker-Vernon Publishing Company, 1911), p. 8-12.

4 William Thompson, grandson of Violet Rinn (Grass Valley, California), Janelle Richardson interviewer, June 26, 2005; audio privately held by Janelle Richardson, Morro Bay, California.

5 1900 U.S. census, Franklin County, Kansas, Williamsburg township, E.D. 93, sheet 2B, dwelling 13, family 43, Lewis Rinn family, Lottie born 30 May 1877, Indian Territory, Claire born 2 Dec 1881[birthdate of Claire incorrect, should be 2 Dec 1879, from U.S., Find a Grave Index], Indian Territory, Daniel Claude born 1 Oct 1881, Indian Territory; digital image *Ancestry.com* (https: www.ancestry.com : accessed 15 Mar 2020); citing NARA microfilm publication T623, roll 480.

6 *The Dodge City Globe* (Kansas). 9 Jul 1878, p. 3; digital images, *newspapers.com* (https: newspapers.com : accessed 10 Mar 2020).

7 Robert Carriker, *Fort Supply, Indian Territory: Frontier Outpost on the Plains* (Norman: University of Oklahoma Press, 1990).

8 *WolframAlpha Computational Intelligence* (https://www.wolframalpha.com/ : accessed 15 Mar 2020).

9 Franklin County, Kansas, Probate Case Files, no. 0718; medical bill 1881, Probate Court clerk's Office, Ottawa, Kansas.

10 *Williamsburg Gazette* (Kansas), 5 Aug 1881, unknown page, Claude Clair posted notice of sale of household goods, photocopy in possession of author.

11 New York The Municipal Archives, death certificate (1881), Claude Clair; Department of Records and Information Center, New York.

12 1900 U.S. census, Franklin County, Kansas, Williamsburg township, E.D. 93, sheet 2B, dwelling 13, family 43, Lewis Rinn family, Claude born 1 Oct 1882, Indian Territory. digital image *Ancestry.com* (https: www.ancestry.com : accessed 15 Mar 2020); citing NARA microfilm publication T623, roll 480.

13 Jessie (Rinn) Spurlin, daughter of Lewis and Marguerite Rinn (Chickasha, Oklahoma), unknown interviewer, prior to 1991; audio privately held by Janelle Richardson, Morro Bay, California.

14 Private letter Leota (Jardon) Hunt to Clair (Rinn) Cole, unknown date. Held in family artifacts of Clair Rinn Cole. Subject of letter shared with Janelle Richardson by email from Paula Phillips unknown date 1990s.

15 1900 U.S. census, Franklin County, Kansas, Williamsburg township, E.D. 93, sheet 2B, dwelling 13, family 43, Lewis Rinn family, Violet Rinn born 25 Feb 1883, Kansas, digital image *Ancestry.com* (https: www.ancestry.com : accessed 15 Mar 2020); citing NARA microfilm publication T623, roll 480.

16 Lewis Rinn Deposit to First National Bank, Ottawa, Kansas, 2 Sept 1882; copy, Jessie Rinn Family artifacts; held by Janelle Richardson.

17 New York The Municipal Archives, death certificate (1881), Claude Clair; Department of Records and Information Center, New York.

18 Franklin County, Kansas, Deeds, 1883-1884, volume 48, p. 67, E.V. Boissiere sold to Lewis Rinn for $1920, July 1883; Register of Deeds, Ottawa, Family History Library microfilm 1,480139.

19 Agreement between Lewis Rinn and Benoite Clair about 1883 for $2500 land improvements at Silkville, document unrecorded; disputed by Benoite 1887-1888, Franklin County, Kansas.

20 1900 U.S. census, Franklin County, Kansas, Williamsburg township, E.D. 93, sheet 2B, dwelling 13, family 43, image 4, Lewis Rinn family, Violet Rinn born 25 Feb 1883, Theoda Rinn born 22 Feb 1885, Lewis Rinn born 26 Dec 1887; digital image *Ancestry.com* (https: www.ancestry.com : accessed 15 Mar 2020); citing NARA microfilm publication T623, roll 488.

21 1885 Kansas state census, Franklin County, population schedule, Williamsburg, p. 9 line 1, dwelling 93, family 116, Lewis Rinn family with Benoite Clair living in household; Kansas State Historical Society, Topeka; microfilm KS1885, roll 50.

22 *WolframAlpha Computational Intelligence* (https://www.wolframalpha.com/ : accessed 15 Mar 2020).

23 "The *American Short-horn Herd Book*," vol 39, (Springfield, Illinois: American Short-horn Breeders Association 1895), p 680. Also "*American Berkshire Record*," vol. 7, (Springfield, Illinois: American Berkshire Association, 1885) p 2014.

24 Franklin County, Kansas, Deeds 1888-89, Volume 64, p. 93, Lewis Rinn sold to E.V. Boissiere, February 1888 for $2358; Register of Deeds, Ottawa, FHL microfilm 1,480147.

25 *WolframAlpha Computational Intelligence* (https://www.wolframalpha.com/ : accessed 15 Mar 2020).

26 Douglas County, Kansas, Marriage Records, 1888, p. 443, image 146, digital image, *Ancestry.com* (https: ancestry.com : accessed 16 Mar 2020). Marriage License Martin Jardan and Theodie Clair.

27 William Cutler, *History of State of Kansas* (Chicago: A.T. Andreaus, 1873) part 10.

28 1900 U.S. census, Franklin County, Kansas, Williamsburg township, E.D. 93, sheet 2B, dwelling 13, family 43, image 4, Lewis Rinn family; Edmond Rinn 29 Jul 1891, Seona Rinn 10 Sep 1893, Jessie Rinn 1 Jan 1896.

29 *Williamsburg Star Newspaper*, 7 December 1887.

30 Franklin County, Kansas, Probate Files, case 0718, 1882-1889, Claude Clair, Ottawa, Kansas.

31 Franklin County, Kansas, Index to Deeds, 1892-1896, Volume 20, p. 97, Swany granted mortgage to Lewis Rinn and wife for Lot 26, Block A, Williamsburg, Kansas, February 1896, released 1900, Register of Deeds, Ottawa, FHL microfilm 1,491315. Also, Franklin County, Kansas, Deeds, 1897-1901, Volume 79, p. 419, Lewis Rinn sold to Margaret Rinn Lot 24, Block A Williamsburg, Kansas, February 1898 for $200 plus $400 mortgage; Register of Deeds, Ottawa, FHL microfilm 1,491310.

32 *Williamsburg Star Newspaper*, 1894-1901, Kansas Historical Society Newspapers on Microfilm; microfilm W274627, April 1900, unknown page.

33 Jessie (Rinn) Spurlin, daughter of Lewis and Marguerite Rinn (Chichasha, Oklahoma), interview by unknown interviewer, prior to 1991; audio privately held by Janelle Richardson, Morro Bay, California.

34 Franklin County, Kansas, Deeds, 1897-1901, Volume 79, p. 419, Lewis Rinn sold to Margaret Rinn Lot 24, Block A Williamsburg, Kansas, February 1898 for $200 plus $400 mortgage; Register of Deeds, Ottawa, FHL microfilm 1,491310.

35 Jessie (Rinn) Spurlin, daughter of Lewis and Marguerite Rinn (Chichasha, Oklahoma), interview by unknown interviewer, prior to 1991.

36 Ibid.

37 1900 U.S. census, Franklin County, Kansas, population schedule, Williamsburg Township, p. 28, E.D. 93, dwelling 43, family 43, Lewis Rinn family.

38 *Williamsburg Star Newspaper*, (Kansas), Oct. 1893 and 1901.

39 *Williamsburg Star Newspaper*, (Kansas), 16 Dec 1898, 21 Dec 1900, 15 Feb 1901, unknown pages.

40 Ibid., 8 Sept 8, 1899, unknown page.

41 Ibid., 8 June, 1900, 29 June 1900, 27 July 1901, p 1.

42 "Ancient Order of United Workmen," article. *Wikipedia*, The Free Encyclopedia, (http://en.wikipedia.org/wiki/Ancient_Order_of_United_Workmen: posted 2 September 2011).

43 *Kansas: a Cyclopedia of State History*, Chicago: Standard Publishing Company, 1912, Volume II, p 80. (http://skyways.lib.ks.us/genweb/archives/1912/k/knights_and_ladies_secur.html: accessed 19 September 2011).

44 Ibid., 7 December 1900.

45 Department of Interior, Bureau of Pensions, pension application, Lewis Rinn, Pvt., Company A, Pennsylvania 62 Inf., 19 July 1890, certificate 612372, National Archives, Washington, D.C.

46 *Williamsburg Star Newspaper* (Kansas), 8 Sept 1899, also 23 Sept, 1899.

47 Emma Estill, *"The Great Lottery: August 6, 1901,"* Chronicles of Oklahoma (http://digital.library.okstate.edu/chronicles/index.html; volume 9: accessed 7May 2012), p 366-381.

48 LR in el Reno, WR July 20, 1901, pg. 1. Also, WR July 20, 1901.

49 Estill, *"The Great Lottery," Chronicles of Oklahoma.*

50 *Williamsburg Republican Newspaper*, 3 Aug 1901 p 1.

51 Jessie (Rinn) Spurlin, interview, prior to 1991.

52 *Williamsburg Republican Newspaper* 17 Aug. 17 1901.

53 Department of Interior, General Land Office El Reno Oklahoma, Homestead Land Patent, Lewis Rinn file, patent file no. 544, (1901-1903); National Archives and Records Administration, Washington D.C.

54 *Williamsburg Republican Newspaper* 7 Sept also 14 Sept 14 1901.

55 Ibid., 2 Nov 1901, pg. 1.

56 Ibid.,2 Nov 1901, pg. 1.

57 Jessie (Rinn) Spurlin, daughter of Lewis and Marguerite Rinn (Chichasha, Oklahoma), interview by unknown interviewer, prior to 1991; audio privately held by Janelle Richardson, Morro Bay, California.

58 *Williamsburg Republican Newspaper,* 23 November 1901.

59 Jessie (Rinn) Spurlin, daughter of Lewis and Marguerite Rinn (Chichasha, Oklahoma), interview by unknown interviewer, prior to 1991; audio privately held by Janelle Richardson, Morro Bay, California.

60 *Williamsburg Republican Newspaper,* 23 November 1901.

61 "Daily Historical Weather Information," *weather.gov* (https:/weather.gov : accessed 30 May 2020).

62 Paula Phillips, "Rinn Family," 1986, private family story based on interviews of Jessie and Seona Rinn, copy held by Janelle Richardson.

63 *Williamsburg Republican Newspaper,* 2 November 1901.

64 Advertisement, *Minco Minstrel Newspaper*, Minco, Oklahoma, March 21, 1902.

65 Jessie (Rinn) Spurlin, interview, prior to 1991.

66 Ibid.

67 Department of Interior, General Land Office El Reno Oklahoma, Homestead Land Patent, Lewis Rinn file, patent file no. 544, (1901-1903); National Archives and Records Administration, Washington D.C.

68 Ibid.

69 Department of Interior, patent certificate 1890 to Lewis Rinn; National Archives and Records Administration, Washington D.C.

70 Department of Interior, certificate of citizenship (1901-1903) to Lewis Rinn; National Archives and Records Administration, Washington D.C.

71 *Williamsburg Republican Newspaper*, 10 September 1903.

72 Helen Mitchell, *Hazel Dell School (1903-1957),* 1996, Minco, Oklahoma. Private publication copy in possession of Janelle Richardson, Morro Bay, California.

73 "Caddo County, Oklahoma," *Wikipedia.org (*https://en.wikipedia.org : accessed 19 April 2020).

74 William Crozier, *Minco Story of a Town*, (W.E. Crozier publisher), 1967. Out of print, copy in possession of Janelle Richardson, Morro Bay, California.

75 Mary Hewett Bailey, "*A History of Grady County, Oklahoma*" (M.A. thesis, University of Oklahoma, 1937).

76 Dixie Gilbert, *Minco, Oklahoma 1890-1990: The First 100 Years,* Minco, Okla.: privately printed.

77 Lewis Rinn private, company A, 62nd Pennsylvania Volunteers, Civil War, certificate no. 612372, Case files of Approved Pension Applications, 1861-1934; Civil War and Later Pension Files; Department of Veteran Affairs, Record Group 15; National Archives and Records Administration, Washington, D.C.

78 Caddo County, Oklahoma, Probate records 1903-1937, Wills, Lewis Rinn 1905; Probate Clerk's Office, Anadarko, Oklahoma, FHL microfilm 2020443, items 1-2.

79 "Obituary Lewis Rinn," (Minco) Oklahoma, *Minco Minstrel Newspaper,* February 24. 1905, p. 1. Lewis Rinn died February 1905.

80 City of Allegheny, Allegheny County, Pennsylvania, death certificate, (1881), Phillip Rinn; The Board of Health, City of Allegheny.

81 *Find a Grave*, (https://www.findagrave.com : accessed 22 April 2020), Hazel Dell Cemetery, Grady County, Oklahoma, Lewis Rinn died 14 Feb 1905. Minco, Grady County, Oklahoma, USA

82 "Obituary Lewis Rinn," (Minco) Oklahoma, *Minco Minstrel Newspaper,* 24 Feb 1905, p. 1. Also, "Knights and Ladies Index to Death Claims," Index. Kansas Historical Society, *Manuscript Collections.* (http://www.kshs.org/p/knights-and-ladies-of-security-security-benefit-association-index-to-death-claims/11316: accessed 19 September 2011).

83 *Evening Herald Newspaper,* Ottawa, Kansas, 24 Feb 1905, p 1, announcement of death of Louis [sic Lewis] Rinn.

84 U.S. Inflation Rate, 1878-2017," *Official Data Compendium, (*https://www.officialdata.org : accessed 23 May 2018.

85 *The Evening Herald*, Ottawa, Kansas, 13 February 1905, p. 2, digital images, *Newspapers.com,* (https:www.newspapers.com : accessed 28 July 2018).

86 Department of Interior, Bureau of Pensions, pension application, Marguerite Clair, widow of Lewis Rinn, Pvt., Company A, Pennsylvania 62 Inf., 28 November 1905, file #147479. National Archives, Washington, D.C.

87 Caddo County, Oklahoma, Will 204 (1905), Lewis Rinn; Probate Court, Caddo, Oklahoma [later transferred to Grady County, Oklahoma].

88 Tarrant County, Texas, marriage records 1817-1965, database on-line, *Ancestry.com* (https"//www.ancestry.com : accessed 8 August 2018), entry for Lottie Rinn and F.S. Pond.

89 Caddo County, Oklahoma, marriage records1890-1995, database on-line, *Ancestry.com* (https"//www.ancestry.com : accessed 8 August 2018), entry for Claire L. Rinn and A.W. Fultz

90 Caddo County, Oklahoma, marriage records1890-1995, database on-line, *Ancestry.com* (https"//www.ancestry.com : accessed 8 August 2018), entry for Violet Rinn and Wm. S. Thompson.

91 Canadian County, Oklahoma, marriage records1890-1995, database on-line, *Ancestry.com* (https"//www.ancestry.com : accessed 8 August 2018), entry for Theoda Wrinn (sp) and W.C. Martin.

92 Garfield County, Oklahoma, marriage records, 1890-1995, database on-line, *Ancestry.com* (https"//www.ancestry.com : accessed 8 August 2018), entry for Claud Rinn and Anna Reeves.

93 Paula Phillips, "Rinn Family History", private paper held by Janelle Richardson, Morro Bay, California.

94 1910 U.S. census, Caddo County, Oklahoma, population schedule, Washington Township, p. 62 (penned), enumeration district (ED) 70, visit 189, family 189, Marguerite Rinn family, Nara microfilm publication T624, roll1245.

95 Ibid.

96 1910 U.S. census, Caddo County, Oklahoma, population schedule, Lone Rock Township, p. 1A, 13, enumeration district (ED) 70, visit 13, family 13, William Gordon household, Lewis Rinn 22 lodger, Nara microfilm publication T624, roll1245.

97 1910 U.S. census, Lane County, Oregon, Eugene Ward 1, p. 23B, ED 163, 822 High Street, visit 491, family 524, Un Pond family, Wife [Lottie] 34, Nara microfilm T624, roll 1283. Also1910 U.S. census, Cowley County, Kansas, Creswell Township, p. 2B, ED 52, dwelling 21, family 21, William Fultz household with Ralph, Clair (sp), and Pauline Fultz, Nara microfilm T624, roll 435. Also 1910 U.S. census, Garfield County, Oklahoma, Enid Ward 2, 602 Ward Street, p. 10A, Ed 8, D. Claude Rinni (sp) household, Nara microfilm T624, roll 1251. Also 1910 U.S. census, Grady County, Oklahoma, Township Ninnekah, ED 104, p. 1A, William and Violet Thompson household, Nara microfilm T624, roll 1252.

98 Canadian County, Oklahoma, marriage records1890-1995, database on-line, *Ancestry.com* (https"//www.ancestry.com : accessed 8 August 2018), entry for Seona Rinn and A.W. Ruel F. Daggs.

99 *Minco Minstrel*, Minco, Oklahoma 13 Nov 1914, Also, 28 April 1911, Also, 23 Aug 1912.

100 *Minco Minstrel*, Minco, Oklahoma, 16 Feb 1912.

101 *Ottawa Daily Republic*, Ottawa, Kansas, 23 July 1913, p. 2, digital images, *Newspapers.com,* (https: www.newspapers.com : accessed 28 July 2018).

102 Douglas County, Kansas, certificate of death, 23611(1917), Benoite Claire (sp) died aged 84; State Board of Health, Topeka, Kansas.

103 Marguerite Rinn (Minco, Oklahoma) to Seona Daggs (Galva, Iowa), letter July 4, 1924; in possession of Janelle Richardson, Morro Bay, California.

104 "Crazy quilting," *Wikipedia (*https://en.wikipedia.org : accessed May 7, 2020).

105 Grady County, Oklahoma, marriage records1890-1995, database on-line, *Ancestry.com* (https"//www.ancestry.com: accessed 8 August 2018), entry for Lewis Rinn and Leoda Sanders.

106 U.S. Department of Veterans Affairs BIRLS Death File, 1850-2010, database on-line, *Ancestry.com* (https://www.ancestry.com : accessed 5 May 2020), Lewis Rinn enrolled 1 Jun 1918, released 11 Feb 1919.

107 Edmond Rinn, "U.S. Transport Service, Passenger Lists," 1918, Records of the Office of the Quartermaster General, NARA Record Group 92, Roll 395.

108 U.S. American Battle Monuments Commission, *American Armies and Battlefields in Europe: A History, Guide and Reference Book*, Washington DC, U.S. Government Printing Office, 1938. Also,
"90th Infantry Division (United States)." *Wikipedia (*http://en.wikipedia : 14 Dec. 2009).

109 Edmond Rinn (Germany) to sister, Violet Rinn Thompson (Oklahoma), letter, 27 January 1919; transcribed copy held in 2009 by Janelle Richardson, Morro Bay, California. He was stationed at Pelm in occupied Germany.

110 Eugene Rinn, youngest son of Edmond Rinn (El Reno, Oklahoma), telephone interview by Janelle Richardson, 13 Dec 2003, "Remembrances of Dad's War Stories", interview notes held by Janelle Richardson, Morro Bay, California.

111 Wilson County, Kansas, certificate of death 103 2084 (1920), Lottie B. Pond; State Board of Health, Topeka, Kansas.

112 Grady County, Oklahoma, marriage records1890-1995, database, *Ancestry.com* (https"//www.ancestry.com : accessed 8 August 2018), entry for Edmond Rinn and Susie Dobbins.

113 Grady County, Oklahoma, marriage records1890-1995, database, *Ancestry.com* (https"//www.ancestry.com : accessed 8 August 2018), entry for Jessie Mae Rinn and Thomas B. Arthur.

114 Marguerite Rinn (Hazel Dell, Oklahoma) to Seona Daggs, (Iowa) letter, 4 July 1924; copy held by Janelle Richardson, Morro Bay, California.

115 Ibid.

116 Oklahoma State Board of Health, Bureau of Vital Statistics, death certificate #26254, Marguerite Rinn, 14 May, Oklahoma City.

117 "Obituary Marguerite Rinn," (Minco) Oklahoma, *Minco Minstrel Newspaper*, 29 May 1924.

118 Ibid.

119 Grady County, Oklahoma, probate record #2127, (June -Nov 1929), Marguerite Rinn, Chickasha, Oklahoma.

120 Saint Etienne, France, Officier de l'etat civil, birth registration, 1857:3E 219/117-119, Marguerite Clair; Archives Departementales de la Loire, Lyon, France.

121 Philippe Chapelin, *Discover Saint Etienne*, Bourg-en-Bresse, France: Editions de la Taillanderie, 1996.

122 "Ribbon and Textiles in Saint Etienne", *Benjamin Arms* (https://www.benjaminarms.com/research : accessed 15 Aug 2019).

123 Saint Etienne, France, Officier de l'etat civil, marriage registration, 1856: 3E 217-219, Claude Clair to Benoite Gonon.

124 Chapelin, *Discover Saint Etienne*. p. 34.

125 Saint Etienne, France, marriage registration, 1856: 3E 217-219, Claude Clair to Benoite Gonon.

126 "Couriot Mine Put Saint Etienne On the Map," Benjamin *Arms* (https://www.benjaminarms.com/research : accessed 15 Aug 2019).

127 Chapelin, *Discover Saint Etienne,* p. 37-40.

128 Ibid.

129 Saint Etienne, France, marriage registration, 1856: 3E 217-219, Claude Clair to Benoite Gonon.

130 Saint Etienne, France, Officier de l'etat civil, birth registration, 1860, Pierre Clair birth; Archives Departementales de la Loire, Lyon, France.

131 *Find a Grave*, database and images (https://www.findagrave.com: accessed 19 Aug 2019), Memorial no. 34352029 for Theodie Jardon, (19 Jan1870-26 Oct 1953), Mount Calvary Cemetery, Baldwin City, Douglas County, Kansas; photo by Mr. Peepers.

132 Saint-Jean-Bonnefonds, France, Officier de l'etat civil, birth registration, 1831: 3E 238/8, Jean Claude Clair; Archives Departementales de la Loire, Lyon, France.

133 Essertines-en-Donzy, France, Officier de l'etat civil, death registration, 1836, Jean Fleury Clair death; Archives Departementales de la Loire, Lyon, France.

134 Saint Etienne, France, Officier de l'etat civil, death registration, 1872: 3E 219/154-156, Marguerite Jacques wife of Francois Gourd death; Archives Departementales de la Loire, Lyon, France.

135 Le Chambon, France, Officier de l'etat civil, birth registration, 1833, 3E 44/6; Benoite Gonon; Archives Departementales de la Loire, Lyon, France. Also Rozier Cotes d' Aurec, France, Officier de l'etat civil, birth registration, 1803 :1M EC 193/2, birth Pierre Gonon; Departementales de la Loire, Lyon, France. Also, Saint Etienne, France, Officier de l'etat civil, death registration, 1871, Pierre Gonon; Departementales de la Loire, Lyon, France. Also, Le Chambon, France, Officier de l'etat civil, birth registration, 1805, Catherine Chapelon; Departementales de la Loire, Lyon, France. Also, Saint Etienne, France, Officier de l'etat civil, death registration, 1890, Catherine Chapelon; Departementales de la Loire, Lyon, France.

136 Paula Phillips, great granddaughter of Marguerite Clair Rinn, Russellville, Arkansas, email to Janelle Richardson, 3 Oct 1999, privately held by Janelle Richardson. Description of 1970s conversation with Jessie Rinn, youngest daughter of Marguerite Clair Rinn, who believed Benoite Gonon Clair's oldest sister was a mother superior.

137 Paula Phillips, Translated French 1914 Obituary for Pierre Forest, privately held by Janelle Richardson. Virginia Forest, nee Virginia Ganon (sp) listed as wife. Mrs. Rinn-Clair listed as family.

138 1880 U.S. census, Osage County, Kansas, Agency township, p. 29 (stamped), dwelling 39, family 40, Antonie Ganon (sp) 46 born in France: image, *Ancestry.com* (https://www.ancestry.com : accessed 20 Aug 2019): citing National Archives microfilm publication T9, roll 391.

139 Cornelia Schrader-Muggenthaler, *The Swiss Emigration Book, Vol. 1,* (Appollo, Pa: Closson Press, 1993) p. 25.

140 Canadian border crossings Ancestry.com. *U.S., Border Crossings from Canada to U.S., 1895-1960* [database on-line]. Lehi, UT, USA: Ancestry.com Operations, Inc., 2010.

Original data: *Records of the Immigration and Naturalization Service, RG 85*. Washington, D.C.: National Archives and Records Administration.

141 1870 U.S. census, Franklin County, Kansas, population schedule, Greenwood Township, p. 76 (stamped), dwelling 49, family 45, Ealton Debosier (sp) head with Claud Claier (sp) family: Digital Image, *Ancestry.com* (https://www.ancestry.com : accessed 22 January 2014); citing NARA microfilm publication M593, roll 434.

142 Customs Service, Record Group 36, "*Passenger Lists of Vessels Arriving at New York, New York (1820-1897), Digital* Image, *Ancestry.com* (https://www.ancestry.com : accessed 11 November 2019); citing NARA microfilm publication *M237, roll 351*, line: *22*, list Number: *1133, image 37*. Also, Le Chambon, France, *Officier de l'etate civil*, birth registration, 1841, Antoinie Gonon born 08 Mar 1841 Le Chambon; Archives Departementales de la Loire, Lyon, France.

143 1880 U.S. census, Osage County, Kansas, population schedule, AgencyTownship, p. 29 (stamped), dwelling 39, family 40, Antonie Gonon blacksmith; Digital Image, Ancestry.com (https://www.ancestry.com : accessed 19 Nov 2019); citing NARA microfilm publication T9, roll559, Image 5.

144 Clyde Thogmartin, "Ernest Valeton de Boissiere and Silkville: The distorted Legacy of a French Philanthropist on the Kansas Frontier, " *The French Review*, 80 (May 6, 2007): 1303-1317, specifically p.1306.

145 Ibid.

146 Lauren Angermayer, "Silkville, Franklin County," *Lost Kansas Communities* (https://lostkscommunities : accessed 4 October 2019).

147 Wikipedia, "Silkville, Kansas," *Wikipedia (*https://en.wikipedia.org : accessed October 4, 2019).

148 Franklin County, Kansas, Probate Case Files, no 0718; land lease, Ealton de Boissier to Claude Clair, 1872, Probate Court clerk's Office, Ottawa, Kansas.

149 Sale of Rinn to de Boissiere

150 Lem Williams, "Silkville in the Early Days," *Franklin County Kansas History* (https://www.franklincokshistory.org : accessed 11 Nov 2019).

151 New York Passenger Lists, 1874, Digital Image, Ancestry.com (https://www.ancestry.com : accessed 11 November 2019); citing NARA microfilm publication M237. Roll 395, List number 1217.

152 Wikipedia, "Ottawa, Kansas," *Wikipedia (* https://en.wikipedia.org : accessed November 11, 2019).

153 Wikipedia, "Leavenworth, Kansas," *Wikipedia (* https://en.wikipedia.org : accessed 5 February 2020).

154 Back of Marguerite Clair photo. Image in possession of Janelle Richardson.

155 Ford County, Kansas, Marriage Certificates, 1876, Lewis Rinn to Marguerite Clair, July 29, 1876, Probate Judge, Dodge City, Kansas; copy held by Janelle Richardson, Morro Bay, California.

156 Garrett R. Carpenter, *Silkville: a Kansas Attempt in the History of Fourierist Utopias, 1869-1892, (*The Emporia State Research Studies, Kansas State Teachers College, Emporia, Kansas, Vol. 3, December, 1954), Number 2, p. 3-31.

157 "M. de Boissiere's Co-operative Farm in Kansas." *The Circular* (Oneida Community, NY), 23 May 1870: 78-79.

158 Clyde, Thogmartin, "Ernest Valeton de Boissiere and Silkville: The distorted Legacy of a French Philanthropist on the Kansas Frontier, " *The French Review*, 80 (May 6, 2007): p. 1303-1317.

159 Carpenter, *Silkville: a Kansas Attempt in the History of Fourierist Utopias, 1869-1892.*

160 *Ottawa Journal (Kansas),* 20 Oct 1870, p. 3, column 2.

161 George Huron, "Ernest Valeton Boissiere," *Transactions of the Kansas State Historical Society*, vol 7 (1902): p. 552-64.

162 Carpenter, *Silkville: a Kansas Attempt in the History of Fourierist Utopias, 1869-1892.*

163 Ibid..

164 Ibid.

165 Ibid.

166 *Williamsburg Gazette (Kansas),* 5 Aug 1881, unknown page, column 2, photocopy in possession of Janelle Richardoson.

167 Franklin County, Kansas, Probate Case Files, no 0718; land lease, Ealton de Boissier to Claude Clair, 1872, Probate Court clerk's Office, Ottawa, Kansas.

168 Carpenter, *Silkville: a Kansas Attempt in the History of Fourierist Utopias, 1869-1892*, p. 28.

169 *The Annals of Kansas* 1886-1910, Vol. I, year 1892, pg 138, Kansas State Historical Society, Topeka, Kansas.

170 Ibid.

171 *Ottawa Weekly Republic* (Kansas), 29 Mar 1894, p. 4, column 4.

172 George Huron, "Erenest Valeton Boissiere," *Transactions of the Kansas State Historical Society* 1901-1902, Vol VII, p.564.

173 Thogmartin, "Ernest Valeton de Boissiere and Silkville," p. 1307.

174 Jennifer McDaniel, Soil Conservation: Williamsburg Ranch Wins Grassland Award, *Ottawaherald.com* (https://www.ottawaherald.com/news/20190202/soil-conservation-williamsburg-ranch-wins-grassland-award : accessed 25 Feb 2020).

175 Kirchenbuch, 1645-1875, Evangelisch Kirche, Heuchelheim, Giessen, Oberhessen, Hesse-Darmstadt, Germany, 1841, No. 20; Family History Library (FHL) microfilm 1,269, 824, Ludwig Rinn, born 21 April 1841, baptized 25 April 1841, parents were Ludwig Rinn and Anna Maria nee Kröck. On the 1900 census, Lewis Rinn stated his birthdate as April 1841. Like his brother, he did not know his exact birthdate.

"Find a Grave Index," database, *FamilySearch* (https://familysearch.org : 13 December 2015), record ID 30136940, *Find a Grave.*

176 Kirchenbuch, 1645-1875, Evangelisch Kirche, Heuchelheim, Germany, 1808; FHL microfilm 1,269, 824, Ludwig Rinn born 3 Mar 1808, Anna Maria Kroeck born 16 April 1808.

177 Kirchenbuch, 1645-1875, Evangelisch Kirche, Heuchelheim, Giessen, Oberhessen, Hesse-Darmstadt, Germany, 1841, No. 20, FHL microfilm 1,269, 824.

178 Kirchenbuch, 1645-1875, Evangelisch Kirche, Heuchelheim, Germany, births 1836, FHL microfilm 1,269, 824. Ludwig Rinn born 27 Oct 1836, died 14 Jul 1837.

179 Konrad Reidt, *Heuchelheim Bei Giessen* (Giessen-Wieseck: Bruhlsche Universitattsdruckerei, 1986, 279.

180 Wikipedia, "Thirty Years' War," article, *Wikipedia*, (https://en.wikipedia.org : accessed July 17, 2020).

181 Telefonbuch 58, 1991/92, Giessen, Wetzlar, Heuchelheim, p. 292.

182 Reidt, *Heuchelheim Bei Giessen,* p. 291.

183 Kirchenbuch, 1645-1875, Evangelisch Kirche, Heuchelheim, Germany, 1808; FHL microfilm 1,269, 824, deaths 1699, Johann Heinrich Rinn died 1699.

184 Kirchenbuch, 1645-1875, Evangelisch Kirche, Heuchelheim, Germany, 1808; FHL microfilm 1,269, 824, 1670 births, Lorenz Kröck born 5 Feb 1670/71.

185 Wikipedia the Free Encyclopedia, "Germany, "article, (https://en.wikipedia.org/wiki/Germany : read 2 August 2018), German Confederation and Empire section.

186 Reidt, *Heuchelheim Bei Giessen,* p. 106.

187 Ibid., p. 60-61.

188 Ibid., p. 313-348.

189 "Passenger Record," database, *New York, Passenger and Crew Lists 1820-1957* (https:// ancestry.com : read 31 August 2018) entry for Jacob Rinn, 20, and Jacob Kroeck arrived 9 July 1849 on the *Oregon.*

190 Helmut Fricke, Burgermeister, Heuchelheim, "Welcome to Heuchelheim, Germany, " presentation to Rinn Descendants, Heuchelheim, Germany, 17 May 2000; photocopy held by Janelle Richardson, Morro Bay, California.

191 Wikipedia the Free Encyclopedia "German revolution of 1848-49," article, (https://en.wikipedia.org/wiki/German_revolutions of 1848-49) : read 31 August 2018.

192 "Passenger Record," database on-line entry for Jacob Rinn, 20, arrived 9 July 1849 on the *Oregon.*

193 Heuchelheim, Giessen, Hesse, Germany, "Listing of town Emigrants", (1849-1855). Copy in possession of Janelle Richardson, Morro Bay, California.

194 "List of Emigrant Names Departing Heuchelheim," archived at Heuchelheim, Germany, museum, Friedrich-Ebert Strasse 9, Heuchelheim, 35452, Germany. Ludwig Rinn IV, listed sheet 5. Printed copy in possession of Janelle Richardson, Morro Bay, California 2019.

195 Manifest, ship *Ocean,* 21 October 1851, Lists Ludwig Rinn family consisting of husband Ludwig (44), Anna Maria wife (44), son Philipp (12), daughter Catherine Elizabeth (18), son Ludwig (10), son Heinrich (8), all from Heuchelheim, digital images *Ancestry.com*, (https://www.ancestry.com : accessed 31 July 2018).

196 "Ports of Embarkation: Bremen and Bremerhaven," article, *Emslanders* (https://emslanders.com) : accessed 31 July 2018.

197 "List of Emigrants Departing Heuchelheim, Germany."

198 Clifford Smith, *German-American Genealogical Research Monograph #25-Letters Home,* "McNeal , Arizona: Westland Publications, 1988.

199 "Record of American and Foreign Shipping," (New York: American Shipmasters' Association, 1880), p. 740.

200 Manifest, ship *Ocean,* 21 October 1851, digital images *Ancestry.com*, (https://www.ancestry.com : accessed 31 July 2018).

201 Dan Rooney and Carol Peterson, *Allegheny City: A History of Pittsburgh's North Side*, Google Books (https://books.google.com/book : read 21 March 2019) (Pittsburgh: University of Pittsburgh Press 2013) p. 22-41.

202 St. Paul's United Evangelical Church (Pittsburgh, Pennsylvania) Church burial records, p. 40; #200, FHL microfilm 1510189 item 6, digital images 7857131, image 790; death listing for Anna Maria Rinn 19 Feb 1852.

203 "A History of Two North Side Congregations," *Archives & Manuscripts* (http://www.pittarchives.tumblr.com : accessed 18 March 2019).

204 Jessie (Rinn) Spurlin, daughter of Lewis Rinn ([Chickasha, Oklahoma]), interview by unknown interviewer 1990s; audio tape privately held by Janelle Richardson, Morro Bay, California.

205 1860 U.S. census, Allegheny County, Pennsylvania, population schedule, Reserve Township, page 63, dwelling 385, family 481, Henry Rinn, butcher, born 1844, Germany, digital images, *Ancestry.com* (https//www.ancestry.com: accessws 2 July 2018); (NARA) microfilm publication M653, roll 1066.

206 1870 U.S. census, Allegheny County, Pennsylvania, population schedule, Ward 7, page 32, dwelling 177, family 234, Henry Peiker, house carpenter, wife Elizabeth age 32, born Germany, digital images, *Ancestry.com* (https//www.ancestry.com: accessed 2 July 2018); (NARA) microfilm publication M593, roll 1291.

207 Lewis Rinn, The Civil War Soldiers and Sailors Database, *National Park Service*, (https://www.nps.gov/civilwar/search-soldiers : read 1 Apr 2019). Lewis Rinn, Private, Company A, 62nd Regiment, Pennsylvania Infantry, Union Army. Citing National archives M554, Roll 102. Also, Lewis Rinn (private, company A, 62nd Pennsylvania Infantry, Civil War), application no. 147479, certificate no. 612372, Case files of Approved Pension Applications, 1861-1934; Civil War and Later Pension Files; Department of Veteran Affairs, Record Group 15; National Archives and Records Administration, Washington, D.C.

208 Jim Murphy, *The Boys' War*, (Clarion Books, New York, 1990), p. 8.

209 Ernest Spisak, *Pittsburgh's Forgotten Civil War Regiment: A History of the 62nd Pennsylvania Volunteer Infantry,* (Tarentum, PA: Word Association, Kindle Edition, 2013) p. 225.

210 The Inflation Calculator, (https://westegg.com/inflation : accessed 4 Apr 2019).

211 Ernest D. Spisak, "The 62ND Pennsylvania Volunteer Infantry," The Gettysburg Magazine: *Historical Articles of Lasting Interest* Issue twenty-six (2002), p. 69-73.

212 Ibid.

213 "Rosters," digital images, Pennsylvania Civil War, *Pennsylvania Volunteers of the Civil War* (http://www.pacivilwar.com : accessed 22 April 2019). 62nd Regiment.

214 Spisak, *Pittsburgh's Forgotten Civil War Regiment: A History of the 62nd Pennsylvania Volunteer Infantry*, p. 341.

215 Ibid. 379.

216 Ibid. 510.

217 Ibid. 597.

218 Ibid. 858.

219 Ibid. 774-776.

220 Ibid. 825.

221 Ibid. 972.

222 Ibid. 1010.

223 Ibid. 1441.

224 Ibid. 2186.

225 Jeffry D. Wert, *The Sword of Lincoln, The Army of the Potomac,* (New York: Simon & Schuster, 2005), p. 53.

226 Ibid.

227 Sisak, *Pittsburgh's Forgotten Civil War Regiment*, p. 2203.

228 Ibid. 2252.

229 Ernest Spisak, *Pittsburgh's Forgotten Civil War Regiment: A History of the 62nd Pennsylvania Volunteer Infantry,* (Tarentum, PA: Word Association, Kindle Edition, 2013), p. 1309.

230 Ibid., 1332.

231 Ibid., 1336.

232 Ibid., 1653.

233 Ibid., 1680

234 Ibid., 1697-1701.

235 Ibid., 2153.

236 Ibid., 3930-4069.

237 Wikipedia, "Taps," *Wikipedia, The Free Encyclopedia,* (https://en.wikipedia.org/ : accessed 30 April, 2019).

238 Spisak, Pittsburgh's *Forgotten Civil War Regiment*, p. 3883.

239 Jeffry D. Wert, *The Sword of Lincoln, The Army of the Potomac,* (New York: Simon & Schuster, 2005), p. 172.

240 "Antietam Sharpsburg," article, American Battlefield Trust, *Civil War Battlefields* (https://www.battlefields.org/learn/civil-war/battles/antietam : accessed 30 April 2019).

241 Spisak, Pittsburgh's *Forgotten Civil War Regiment*, p. 4212.

242 Ibid., 4203.

243 "The True Battle for Fredericksburg," article, American Battlefield Trust, *Civil War Battlefields* (https://www.battlefields.org/learn/articles/true-battle-fredericksburg : accessed 13 May 2019).

244 Ibid.

245 Henry Rinn (private, company B, 123 Pennsylvania Infantry, Civil War), application no. 1296263, certificate no. 1060434, Case files of Approved Pension Applications, 1861-1934; Civil War and Later Pension Files; Department of Veteran Affairs, Record Group 15; National Archives and Records Administration, Washington, D.C. Also Phillip Rinn (private, company B, 123 Pennsylvania Infantry, Civil War), certificate no. 374243, Case files of Approved Pension Applications, 1861-1934; Civil War and Later Pension Files; Department of Veteran Affairs, Record Group 15; National Archives and Records Administration, Washington, D.C.

246 Lewis Rinn (private, company A, 62nd Pennsylvania Infantry, Civil War), pension application no. 147479, certificate no. 612372, Case files of Approved Pension Applications, 1861-1934; Civil War and Later Pension Files; Department of Veteran Affairs, Record Group

247 "An army marches on its stomach," definition, *Dictionary.com* (https://www.dictionary.com : accessed 18 May 2019).

248 "Food," article, *Civil War Saga* (http://civilwarsaga.com : accessed 18 May 2019).

249 Ibid.

250 "Civil War Food," article, *Civil War Academy* (https://www.civilwaracademy.com : accessed 18 May 2019).

251 Ibid.

252 Spisak, Pittsburgh's *Forgotten Civil War Regiment*, p. 5179-5256.

253 Ibid., 5556-5787.

254 Jim Murphy, *The Boy's War,* (New York: Clarion Books, 1990), p. 49-51.

255 Spisak, Pittsburgh's *Forgotten Civil War Regiment,* p.6065-6157.

256 Ibid., 6577-6635.

257 Ibid., 7371.

258 Stephen Ambrose, *Halleck: Lincoln's Chief of Staff,* (Baton Rouge: LSU Press, 1996), p. 142.

259 " 62nd Regiment, Pennsylvania Infantry," article, *National Park Service* (https://www.nps.gov/civilwar : accessed 21 May 2019).

260 Wikipedia, "62nd Pennsylvania Infantry Regiment, *Wikipedia.org.* (https://en.wikipedia.org/wiki/62nd_Pennsylvania : accessed 21 May 2019.).

261 Spisak, Pittsburgh's *Forgotten Civil War Regiment*, p. 9753.

262 Lewis Rinn (private, company A, 62nd Pennsylvania Infantry, Civil War), pension application no. 147479, certificate no. 612372. Also Inflation Calculator, *Westegg.com.* (https://westegg.com/inflation : accessed 21 May 2019).

263 No records found for Ludwig Rinn sr. (born 1808 Germany) or any individual resembling him. Search involved 1860 and 1870 census search for Pennsylvania and surrounding states including a "line by line" examination of 1860 Allegheny City. Also search of Allegheny City St. Paul's Church burial records and marriage records, 1850-1890. Allegheny County and Pennsylvania Naturalization records, probate records, death records.

264 Wikipedia, "Pittsburgh in the American Civil War," *Wikipedia, (*https://en.wikipedia.org/ : accessed June 23, 2019).

265 Wikipedia, "History of Pittsburgh," *Wikipedia, (*https://en.wikipedia.org/ : accessed 23 June 2019).

266 Lewis Rinn (private, company A, 62nd Pennsylvania Infantry, Civil War), application no. 147479, certificate no. 612372, Case files of Approved Pension Applications, 1861-1934; Civil War and Later Pension Files; Department of Veteran Affairs, Record Group 15; National Archives and Records Administration, Washington, D.C.

267 Garver, Bruce, "Immigration to the Great Plains, 1865-1914 war, politics, technology, and economic development," *Great Plains Quarterly* (Summer 2011), digital edition, *Digital Commons University of Nebraska, (*http://digitalcommons.unl.edu : accessed 23 June 2019), p. 179-203.

268 Wikipedia, "Main Line Pittsburgh to St. Louis," *Wikipedia,* (https://en.wikipedia.org/ : accessed 17 June 2019).

269 Wikipedia, "Eads Bridge," *Wikipedia,* https://en.wikipedia.org (accessed July 8, 2019).

270 "St. Louis, Missouri Population," *World Population Review,* (http://worldpopulationreview.com/us-cities : accessed 23 June 2019).

271 Missouri Marriage Records, 1805-2002, Henry Rinn to Anna Marie Osten 1867; Missouri State Archives; Jefferson City, Missouri; database, *Ancestry.com* (http://ancestry.com : accessed 24 June 2019).

272 "Indian Territory," The Columbia Encyclopedia, *Encyclopedia.com* (https://www.encyclopedia.com/territory : accessed 17 June 2019).

273 Ford County, Kansas; consulted as "Ford County Marriage Records 1874-1880," *Ancestry.com* (http://ancestry.com : accessed 24 June 2019).

274 Jessie (Rinn) Spurlin, daughter of Lewis and Marguerite Rinn (Chichasha, Oklahoma), unknown interviewee, prior to 1991; audio privately held by Janelle Richardson, Morro Bay, California.

275 Wikipedia, "Fort Supply," *Wikipedia* (https://en.wikipedia.org : accessed 17 June 2019).

www.ingramcontent.com/pod-product-compliance
Lightning Source LLC
Chambersburg PA
CBHW061225150426
42811CB00057BB/1273